My Journey To
Finding Faith

ORLA
KELLY
PUBLISHING

Chris Morgan

Orla Kelly Publishing
27 Kilbrody,
Mount Oval,
Rochestown,
Cork,
Ireland.

Acknowledgement

I am dedicating this book to Spirit and am very grateful for the lovely magical moments I have experienced over the last twenty years, meeting such beautiful people and being part of their lives.

I want to thank my Guides, one of whom was my uncle, my father's brother, who passed to the spirit world over twenty-five years ago. I would get a vision of his face when he would talk to me, and he has always been an inspiration.

I would also like to thank Carter for being another Guide when I started my spiritual journey and seeing his face light up with such beautiful features. Another Guide, her name is Maria, and she is a nun. As a teenager, I always loved the song *Maria*; I was always singing it. When I asked my Guide her name, I could hear the song, Maria. I just met a girl called Maria.

I want to thank Merlin, another one of my Guides. Many of you would know him as the Wizard from Camelot. I want to thank all the Angels and beings of light who have helped me with their divine guidance throughout my life. I am eternally grateful.

I would also like to thank my friends Trish for typing the book and Theresa and Diana for helping with the book and for Paul Chute for the gift of the cover design.

I hope readers will enjoy the magical divine intervention in the many stories written. I do hope it opens the door to Spirituality for you all. God bless all who come on this journey with me to read this book.

About The Author

I first became interested in Angels and Spirit Guides when I attended a meditation class where I met healers, psychics, and mediums. They would often channel Angels and Spirit Guides, and I was fascinated by spirituality. It was all so new to me. I didn't believe in any religion. I didn't have any faith, but I could feel an energy. It is a vibration if you don't understand what an energy is. It can feel as light as a feather. Another way to explain it is it's like going to a surprise party, and all the excitement with music playing loud, and the atmosphere is electrifying. That's also a vibration, and energy can be any vibration, either light or heavy.

I felt a strong connection with Angels. The healers I had spoken to all did healing on each other to free up their bodies from emotional stress. I started doing healing courses, and I was able to join the group and give healing and receive healing. We did a lot of healing over time to release all emotional stress from our bodies.

I did a lot of healing on spiritual growth and personal development, and over time, I felt more inner peace and confidence in myself, and I felt my body become lighter. It was so powerful.

I am writing this book now because Spirit asked me to. They have been asking me to write this book for years, and I just never got around to it. Then Spirit came one day, and I could tell they were unhappy with me. They said, "For twenty years, we have been asking you to write a book bringing people into your life, making connections." They told me they are all short stories and need to be written. Now I have written the book. Sorry Spirit, it has taken so long.

First, Spirit shows me the connections they have made by meeting all the amazing people I have met. I feel very blessed to be part of their journey. Hopefully, this will bring an awareness that Angels and Guides are here with us.

I hope the readers will connect with the messages from Spirit through all the short stories. Most especially connect with the amazing little miracles, such as the highly evolved being that came on the planet to work from Heaven, the story about the master of ceremonies, and how the Angel stepped into my body to work on people at the dinner dance in the hotel. I hope the reader can see how powerful they are. I hope they realise that there is no coincidence. Everything happens for a reason.

We are spiritual beings in human bodies here on the Earth to experience human emotions, and we are a journey of souls, able to connect and learn from other souls. Planet Earth is the school of life. Once we learn and complete the lessons, we return to God. Our souls hold the lessons and everything we have learned on earth.

I am eternally grateful to Spirit in my life but I always felt something was missing, and I just couldn't put my finger on it. Once I could connect with Spirit in myself, everything fitted, and I felt complete in myself. Unfortunately, I did not connect with Spirit till I was forty years on the planet. I wish I could have connected with Spirit as a child. It would have empowered me to be stronger much earlier in my life.

Having awareness is the key to connecting with Spirit. There are Angels for everything, and Divine guidance is always there. All we have to do is call on the Angels and Spirit Guides or just call on Spirit to invite them into our life and ask for whatever we wish. There are Angels for car parking spaces, help with exams, dream jobs, a husband or a wife, creativity, and writing. If you surrender and trust Spirit, hand your life over and ask if you can learn the lessons quickly and have a better life.

If you surrender your life completely to Spirit, the Angels will support and help you in your journey.

By surrendering to Spirit, you can achieve all. Angels will open doors in your life to opportunities. Just trust. They have never let me down. Always thank Spirit, the Angels and the Guides and hand over whatever you would like in your life. And wait and see what happens. I am very grateful to Spirit for the journey they brought me on.

viii

Contents

Spirit Was Showing A Sign

I looked forward to going to Spain and passed a bookshop at the airport. I thought about buying a book to read on the plane, so as I walked in, I went straight to the Spiritual section. There was this young girl about twenty-one years old in there who kept looking at me. I greeted her and as I looked at the books, I asked if she could recommend one as there were so many. We started chatting about books in general.

As she looked at me, I felt she wanted to ask me something; it was like a question of wonder in her eyes. I thought she was a bit shy, so I just told her, "I feel you want to ask me a question." She stared at me for a few minutes. I said, "What is it you want to ask?" I told her people get brought together for a reason, usually for answers to questions we don't know how to ask.

She said "I do have a question. Did you come in here to tell me something?" I said I would ask Spirit if there was a message for her. Then I said, Spirit has been showing you colours, pictures, and visions, and you're trying to figure out what's happening to you as sometimes you feel it's a bit crazy.

The Angels told me you have a psychic gift and then went on to say your third eye is opening. They are also telling me they told you to wait in this shop.

Then she said "Oh My God, that's true. I have been wondering what was happening to me. Then I heard a voice saying someone would tell me what was happening. Wait until someone comes into the shop, everything will be explained to you, and you will get an answer. Don't fear. All will be okay, and you will understand."

Marg Minding Her Friend

Marg rang me out of the blue, telling me she had this friend who wanted to kill herself and thought of me for advice.

I could see her mind in confusion. She seemed quite stressed. She said she had overspent because she was going through a lot of petrol, collecting her friend and taking her back and forth to work.

Marg was renting an apartment and told me she didn't have money to get through the last few days of the week. She was wondering how she was going to eat. I offered her money to help, and she wouldn't take it and said she had to go.

I said "You must take your friend to a doctor as she needed professional help. She is suffering from mental health issues, and she was traumatized."

After she left, I asked the Angels "What can I do to help her. She won't take money from me." The Angels said, "Give her fifty euro in a card, write this verse, and give it to her."

From The Angels Above,
To Our Angel Below,
In Our Hearts, We Love You So,
This Is Sent With Love And Best Wishes
With Abundance Of Hugs And Lots Of Kisses.

I called to Marg's workplace, gave her the card, and told her it was a message from the Angels, and I left quickly before she could open it.

Later that morning she texted me saying that her Angels never let her down. She was so grateful and thanked me for passing on the message. She felt her faith was empowered when she read the card.

A Fireplace

I wanted a new fireplace, but they were so expensive. I looked everywhere and was saying to the Angels how was I going to afford one. I could hear the Angels telling me I would get a brand new fireplace from a big house that had never been used by a builder who built the house. The house would be up a hill with turrets on the roof of the builder's house.

I went shopping with my father, bought the evening paper, and gave it to him, asking him to look up the advertisements on the paper and see what fireplaces were for sale. I had taken the measurements hoping to get one soon.

I had told my father the story about my vision of buying the fireplace from the builder, but he didn't believe me. Dad saw a mahogany fireplace for sale with a phone number.

We rang the number, and the man who answered told me I was the first call he received and he gave me his address and directions to his house.

We went to the house, and like I was told, he lived in a big house on a hill with a turret on the roof of his home. He bought us into his house to show us the fireplace and told me I was lucky as it had never been used.

We agreed on a price and he was a very honourable man. I asked him if he was a builder, and he said yes. You should have seen my father's face. He was stunned. The builder said he would take out the fireplace that night and asked if I could get someone to collect it the next day.

A friend of mine was doing painting in my home. He had a big lorry and did deliveries part-time. I was telling him about getting the fireplace from a builder that was never used. He said "Don't be ridiculous that's not going to happen", but his wife said "I believe it will happen, Spirit looks after Chris."

He just walked away saying he didn't believe it would happen, and he had better things to do than listen to us talking nonsense.

I told the builder the name of my friend who would collect the fireplace, and he said he knew him as he did deliveries for the builder. They knew each other. What are the chances of that?

It was collected the next day, and the builder told my friend how I was lucky to get a fireplace that had never been used. My friend looked at me and looked back at the builder. You could see he was well shocked. I smiled at him and said "Now you believe in my Angels, don't you?" He just said "You are weird" as he didn't believe in Angels. I reminded him that maybe he should start; how else did I get this fireplace? He thinks I am strange now. I just smiled and said "Maybe you should have a little faith!"

Women In Wilton

Back in 1995, I took care of my friend's two boys while she went shopping for her sister's wedding. I was taking one of the little boys to the bathroom. and while I was on my way, I saw a woman in her late sixties also heading to the bathrooms with a friend and she had a very strange look on her face.

I just had a powerful feeling that I should wait until she exited the bathroom. As she came out, she started saying "I'm falling; I'm falling." She was falling to the ground and holding her friend's coat as she slowly ended up on the floor.

There were two entries into those bathrooms and a constant flow of people. I then told everyone to shut those doors and call security and an ambulance. The woman was turning blue, but no one had called an ambulance. I shouted again. "Call an ambulance; this is an emergency."

Everything was happening so fast. I started CPR on this woman, which seemed to take a long time. I could see where the blue was on one side of her face, and it slowly started to fade, and her colour was coming back very slowly. Then a woman came out of the crowd, saying she was a nurse.

I was so glad to see her. We worked on the women together. After a while, the ambulance came. I was telling the paramedic what had happened, and he said it was always good to have CPR. I told him I was watching the breakfast morning program on the television, where they showed how to save a life. He told me I kept the woman alive with my quick action. I felt better when the nurse came and I was sad I never got her name.

The ambulance went away with the lady, and they had her on oxygen. Thankfully, she appeared to be ok. As they left, I burst out crying and started shaking, thinking about what had happened. Within an hour or two, I rang the hospital to see how the woman was. I spoke to a lovely nurse. She had heard from the paramedic what I had done and asked if I wanted to come to the hospital. as the woman was doing great. Her brother was a priest, and her sister, a nun. They were both there with her. I had issues with religion back in those days and didn't have any faith; nor believe there was a God.

I wish I had gone to meet them. Looking back, I wasn't open to Spirit in my life. I have always regretted not meeting her family.

The Little Ascended Master

My cousin minded this little boy Denis and his two brothers. There was just something about Denis. I always felt he was a special, kind, thoughtful child, just a beautiful soul. I often saw him when I called my cousin's house.

One day I went with my cousin to collect the children from school. I noticed Denis was a bit sad and down in himself. His parents worked long hours, and he missed them both.

On the way home, we stopped as my cousin wanted to go shopping. I waited in the car with Denis as he hated shopping. I was chatting with him, and he started telling me he could remember being in his mummy's tummy and the conversations his mum and dad would have. He said he didn't like being in his mum's tummy as he didn't like how it felt when his mum and dad would fight. He was so sensitive to energy.

He said he didn't feel wanted or loved; he just wanted to be loved. I tried to assure him that mums and dads must work to pay the bills and would prefer to stay home with their children. We became good friends, and I would always tell him he was a special boy because he had such a kind, thoughtful heart filled with compassion and love.

Many years before, Spirit told me I would carry ascended master energy for a very powerful child, a little boy. I thought it might be that I would have a powerful child, but I never had children, only to later find out the energy was for Denis. Spirit told me the energy had been transferred to Denis.

Often when we both would chat, I felt I needed to pass positive thoughts on using energy. His brother sometimes bullied him, and he often cried about it. I told him I would teach him magic.

I told him to close his eyes, say the magic words *Abracadabra*, and focus on his brother having a great heart full of love and kindness. I told him his brother wanted to be nice and just needed some help.

Closing our eyes, we would visualize his brother being kind, caring and full of love. He would be nice to everyone forever, and even though he was sometimes horrible, he had a good heart, but he didn't know it, and because Denis had powers, he could see it.

Another time I told him that he was so lucky to have a mum and dad. What about all the boys and girls in the world who didn't have a mum or a dad, and some kids had no parents at all?

We would close our eyes together, saying the magic word *Abracadabra* and ask God to help all the kids worldwide and send mums and dads to them all. We would always turn negative things into positive things because things would change when he asked for them. After all, God is the magic, and it is important always to have good powerful thoughts. I told him he had the positive power always to do great things.

When his Ascending Master energy grows with him, he will have a little understanding of his power as he grows and becomes the Ascending Master he truly is. I didn't see him anymore as his family moved out of the area, but I will never forget him. God bless him on his journey as Spirit guides him.

We Asked For A Sign

I went on a Mediumship course in Bandon a long time ago. I was learning how it all worked, as I was very curious. When one is doing Mediumship, everything has to be verified. The teacher was connecting with her family, who passed away, and the teacher asked me to communicate with her uncle.

I started seeing lots of big carrots, boots, and a man sitting on a chair, putting wood on a stove. It was one of those big ranges people would have in the country. I saw glasses and a mug of tea on the stove.

She then told me her uncle was a farmer and was very proud of his carrots, they were huge, and he wore boots on the farm and always sat on a chair by the stove drinking tea and reading the paper.

Later in the afternoon, we started doing Mediumship with our Angels and Guides. We asked the Angels and Guides to prove they were in the room. We asked them to do something that we could see. The teacher was playing a CD with vocals on it, so we sat there and asked to show us something.

Nothing appeared to happen, but then we decided to do a meditation. The teacher played the music again, but this time, Spirit had taken the singer's voice off the CD with just music in the background. We all looked at each other. This music was the same track that had earlier had vocals.

Visiting Mother Amma

Many years ago, I went to visit Mother Amma for the Darshan. You have to queue early morning to get tickets.

Mother Amma is a beautiful Indian lady. She is very powerful and has a gift of bringing up everybody's stress and issues to release. It's healing. She is an embodiment of Christ.

You can feel love energy in the hall where she is. Her presence is amazing. A lot of people sit in her presence for many hours. While there, I told my friends I would love to go for a second Darshan. But I wasn't staying the next day. I spoke to Amma in meditation and asked if there was any way I could have another Darshan. I felt an amazing connection and, for some reason, thought I needed to return to her. I sensed it just felt unfinished.

Within about ten minutes, one of the girls selling tickets came over to me and asked me to go and sell tickets, and when I finished, I gave the bag of money and tickets to another lady who was over by a stand.

As I walked away, my friend walked towards me and we started to chat. I became aware of something on the ground, and there was a ticket right between us. The ticket was opened as it lay on the ground, and we both looked at it. I looked up to see what number was next in the queue, and the ticket I found was to see Amma. How wonderful!

My friend said "That ticket is for you. Go and see Amma." Well! I was thrilled. I told Amma that this ticket was really for me, and I heard, "Thank you for selling the tickets." I was amazed.

There are lots of stalls where you can buy photos and jewellery that Mother Amma has worn, and her healing energy would be on it. Months before that I kept hearing that I would buy a plain ring. I didn't know where I would get it at the time as I didn't think I wanted a ring. While looking at all Mother Amma's clothes, jewellery, photos and Indian gifts, I saw a plain band. I tried it on, and it fitted. Then I heard, "Buy the ring. It will help you in your life and your mother's grief," so I bought it. Of course, Mother Amma's energy is beautiful, and I wear it all the time now. I feel it brings me great peace.

Later that evening, my friend and I went to the airport to fly home. While I was on the plane coming home, Mother Amma came to me and said "Thank you for coming to see me." That just made my day even more. I felt so blessed. What an amazing day I had.

Another time when I had gone to see Mother Amma, a woman came to see me while I was standing in the queue. She offered me a chair. She said she knew that I found it difficult to stand. I felt grateful as I was struggling to stand and walk.

While visiting Mother Amma, I met a young girl I had met twice before that. She knew a friend of mine. She was struggling with addiction and was telling me that she was going to Dublin. The Angels told me she was going to Dublin to end her life. Her brother lived in Dublin and could take care of everything once she was gone.

She had it all planned. She was going to jump from a bridge. I felt so sorry for her. How could I stop her from committing suicide? She knew I had great faith in the Angels, so I told her it was a good thing we met. I told her I knew why she was going to Dublin and mentioned I knew about the bridge she planned to jump off.

I could see from her face that she was very shocked, so I told her that before we came down to this earth, our return journey to Heaven was planned, and we were here to learn lessons. Once we have learnt the lessons, then we go back to Heaven. I told her that we don't get another flight if we don't get on that flight. I said, "Once you commit suicide, you walk the earth for thousands of years with all the killers and bad people you can think of. You will see all your family for generations, born, live and die, and you will be scared forever, and there is no way back."

I had to scare her into staying alive. "Go and do counselling, and face your fears. It's a lot easier to do this. Become a strong person and help others to live. You can make a difference and save lives." What an amazing lesson to learn, and she did. She turned her life around.

I met her in Dublin years later. She came up, put her arms around me, and told her friends that I was the woman she had spoken about and I had saved her life.

She was in tears thanking me, and I was in tears, too. I reminded her that all I did was point her to a spiritual door and she walked through it herself.

I could hear Mother Amma say "Thank you for saving her life." I was so grateful to hear Mother Amma say that. It was so emotional. As I write this, it still makes me feel emotional today.

Meeting My Guide And Guardian Angel

The third eye is in the middle of the forehead. It's like watching television but seeing into the future. It is very powerful. The people we see are people in our lives or who will come into our lives. Our third eye is connected to our Solar Plexus where it gives you your gut feeling. When you sense something is right or wrong, always trust your feeling, it's a way Spirit guides us.

When my third eye started to open, I saw black and white dots. After a while, I began to see the colour green which symbolising heart energy.

Then weeks later, I saw Angel wings. It takes a long time for your third eye to open properly. Later, I saw another Angel. He had a lovely face. It glowed with bright white light. He told me he was one of my Guides. I was just fascinated he would talk to me. I asked him his name. He said his name was Carter. I always felt a strong sense of peace when I saw him.

A Highly Evolved Soul

One of my friends, Kim, is a midwife, and while we were chatting over coffee, I was getting a message from Spirit, that they wanted me to ask her if it would be okay to use her body to channel energy.

She was delighted to be asked and immediately surrendered to whatever Spirit wanted to do through her. I channelled energy into her. It turned into a pyramid shape three times, one folding into the other and entering her solar plexus area.

When I asked Spirit what this energy would do, I saw a hand trying to fit into a glove, but I felt that the hand couldn't get into the glove.

A few weeks later, Kim called me. Something amazing happened that very morning. A baby girl was born, and as she lay there, she was lifeless. Kim is very sensitive to energy and is a Reiki Master. Kim felt a strong pull of energy from her solar plexus as she tried to connect with the baby, and after a while, the energy was so powerful, coming through her solar plexus to the baby. Through this magnetic force of life energy, she started to see the change in the baby and the baby started to respond.

Then she told me the baby had Down Syndrome and other medical problems. The baby was very weak.

Kim said she was just a beautiful little girl whose parents adored her.

A few months passed, and the baby girl was still weak and holding on. We called her Baby Angel because she was very beautiful. Baby Angel was now six months, spending much time in the hospital. Then she started having trouble, and she began to get weaker and weaker. Kim rang me, saying Baby Angel would not live through the night.

I asked Spirit what I could do to help Baby Angel. I felt guided to ask Kim to call into Baby Angel at three o'clock, as Christ died at three, a very powerful time to send healing. I called on every Angel in Heaven, every being of Light, to help Baby Angel.

I handed her over and kept asking for help. I told Kim that I didn't feel it was her time to go. I felt she should be here another few months. Spirit had told me she was doing work on the planet and that she needed to stay to finish whatever work she had to do. At that time, I didn't know what the work was while healing was going on with Baby Angel.

Kim was in the room talking with the nurses, and Baby Angel's breathing started to get stronger and stronger before her eyes. The nurses were thrilled and thanked God for Baby Angel. She got better and didn't need the life support machine anymore. About eight weeks later, Kim rang me crying. Baby Angel had taken a turn for the worst. Spirit told me it was her time to go home; her work was done. It was so sad. Just remembering her brings tears to my eyes. Baby Angel left this world and went home.

Kim said Baby Angel's removal was the next night. Her mum had bought her the most beautiful pink dress with ribbon and bows. They brought her to the church in a little white coffin. Baby Angel's mum and dad would leave her in the church overnight when the service was over, as that usually happens.

The priest was wonderful. He said "Why would you leave her in the church. She is only a baby. Take her home and bring her back in the morning."

Kim called to me that night. She had seen Baby Angel. She said she looked so beautiful and peaceful, like she was asleep.

I had a lovely candle, and Spirit told me to put the energy of compassion and love into the candle. Spirit said "While it burns, leave it to burn to the end. It was to help the parents with their grief."

That night I was sitting down watching TV. Our Lady came to me with Baby Angel. Our Lady asked me if I wanted to hold Baby Angel in my arms. I was very honoured; what a privilege. The minute I held her in my arms, I felt shivers shooting up my body for over half an hour.

I was stunned. I was holding the energy of a very special being of light doing the work on the whole planet. What a miracle. It was the most amazing feeling, and I am so grateful to hold Baby Angel's energy. We all knew she was special; but we didn't know how much. All those who met Baby Angel were truly blessed.

A year passed, and Baby Angel's mum was pregnant again, this time with twins. Everybody was thrilled with such great news. Some of the nurses said to Baby Angel's mum, Baby Angel had to go back to bring another baby. Now she has beautiful babies, a healthy boy and a girl.

I asked Christ that night whether Baby Angel needed help getting to the spirit world. I was told she was with Christ and then I got a vision. She was kicking off her body like you would throw off your shoes.

That night I asked Christ and the Angels what work Baby Angel was doing here. Then I heard "Why don't you ask me?" in a cheeky voice. It was Baby Angel herself. She told me to imagine everybody on the planet with a square shape of sharp energy around them. She put a circle around everyone to soften everyone's energy on the planet, to help the planet for Ascension.

As the planet went from the 3rd to the 5th Dimensions, it was to prepare everyone on Earth for the Unveiling of the Planet in 2012.

Spirit said Baby Angel is a very highly evolved vibration being of light, and when it was time for Baby Angel to be born, she needed angelic help to get into the baby's body. The angels got Kim ready with an electronic magnetic pyramid energy field to suction the highly evolved being of light to be grounded in the baby's body to do all the work needed on the planet.

Spirit asked me to contact Kim and ask her to call after the funeral. When she called over to me, I saw three pyramids come out of her Solar Plexus soar, smash into tiny bits of energy in the air, and disappear. That was amazing to see.

Spirit had a message for Kim. Christ and Our Lady came channelling through me and thanked Kim for all she did holding the energy. Christ and Our Lady were so humble and grateful to Kim. We were just shocked to hear them. Nothing could have prepared me to experience such a miracle. When I think of that time, I can only say that it was a pure blessing.

For years, Kim would say she would love to meet a nice man, get married, and have two children. That was her dream and a house in the country, and at thirty-five, she didn't think it would happen. I am delighted to say all her dreams came through. She has a handsome man, two beautiful children and a home in the country.

The Angels told me Kim would get the blessings she wanted, and she did. It was a whirlwind romance.

A Gateway To My Tummy

Many years ago - I think around 2005, I went on a healing course. One evening when we had finished our course, a few of us were chatting after dinner, and the Angels asked if they could put an energic gateway in my tummy.

As new baby energy would connect with mother's love before they were conceived into their biological mothers. All the Angels entered the room and started creating a Gateway for the babies' energy to pass through, like a Stargate, which some of you have seen in science fiction films. I lay there for 45 minutes while this was happening, feeling very privileged that they were doing this to me. I was told many babies would pass through this energic Gateway.

I could feel the Angels cutting into my tummy. We could see sparkling energy around me. While this was happening, it didn't hurt. I just felt all these different sensations. Then when they had finished, they stitched my energy together. The same as if they were stitching anyone up. Amazing psychic surgery.

Being Spiritual is very magical.

Care Assistant In The Hospital

There was a care assistant in the hospital that I felt drawn to, to give a message. Spirit said she was to do her training and become a nurse, everything would go her way, and work out.

She told me that since she was twenty, she had wanted to become a nurse. She was the youngest in the family, and her father wouldn't let her travel to London to do a nursing course.

She has been looking after various family members for thirty years, as she loved caring for people. She was now in her fifties, and her family had grown up. Now it was her time.

Spirit thanked her for all the care she has given over the years and that they wanted her to become a nurse now. Spirit said she would do it in Cork and to trust.

She felt shivers through her body when I gave her personal messages. A lovely woman with a heart of gold who was very grateful for the message. She said it all meant so much. She got her nursing course in Cork.

Michael Jackson And The Spirit World

Years ago, I was out to lunch with my psychic friend. We were chatting, and I saw a white glove with a hand in it. I asked her if she saw or felt anything here, and she nodded. We both said together that it was Michael Jackson. What a lovely surprise. He had passed a few weeks before.

I told him not to be afraid. I would help him pass over to the Spirit world, and he would be okay. Seeing him standing tall, I started to get a flash of his energy. We both looked at each other, saying "Oh my God, Michael Jackson." He had such beautiful, gentle energy. It was pure, unconditional love. I felt very privileged to help pass him on to the Spirit world.

The Carpet Man

When my husband and I separated many years ago, I moved back to my house. A man came to clean the carpet and asked me if I believed in life after death? He told me his baby daughter passed, and he often felt her around him, and she spoke quite often to him.

I asked him if he would like to feel his baby girl's energy? The Angels came and put her into his arms. He could feel her. He said "I can feel the weight of her." I said, "Say whatever you want to tell her." He had a chat with her and there were tears in his eyes. He said it was a beautiful experience. I then asked if giving her back to the Angels was okay. An Angel took the baby back. He could feel the Angel taking his baby girl from him.

He told me he heard three words an hour before, and wrote them down. He said he didn't think the message he got was for himself and asked if he could show it to me. The words were Believe, Trust, and Achieve. That was just what I needed to hear at the time.

Moving House With An Unexpected Visit

In one of my visions, I saw myself at a round table, sitting with many people I didn't know. The table had a buffet of beautiful food. I saw what looked like a bowl of potato salad with parsley. I sensed it was in the countryside.

I often wondered what it would be like to live in the countryside, with nature on your doorstep. I started looking at houses to rent and saw a house that reminded me of a drama program on TV years ago called 'Upstairs Downstairs.' It was a really lovely house.

I decided to rent the house and two insurance guys called; an older man and a younger guy, about twenty. I could hear a voice saying to ask him about his mother and how she was. I didn't want to ask. "Just ask him now." There was a force about how it came out of me as I didn't want to say it. Then looking at me with wonder in his eyes, he said, "Why did you ask me that?" Then I heard a voice in my head, "Tell him to ask his Mum to come and see you."

I told him I was getting a message from Spirit for his Mum to come and see me but they were not telling me why, so I would have to wait and see what happens.

Three weeks later his Mum phoned me, and she asked me who I was. She said that this was all very strange. I explained that I struggled with saying anything, and Spirit pushed it out of my mouth.

While chatting, she asked for directions to the house I had moved into. As I gave her the directions, she said, "Is that house called Sahara House?" I told her it was and confirmed she knew how to get here. She said that house was her family home, her mother's house. Both of us were stunned, and we both said "Oh my God."

She started telling me about the house and how a long time ago, a doctor had lived in that house, and priests lived there as there was a little church and a graveyard. The priests would have their garments, which they would say mass in, all hanging in the room next to the kitchen. And when you would walk into this room, there was the most beautiful calm, peaceful feeling.

I remember the first time I drove up the driveway to this house. It was a very eerie feeling. It felt like fear, just uncomfortable, like going back in time. That's the best way to explain it.

When this lovely lady came to see me, she brought cooking apples and a tea towel as a house warming gift, as I had only recently moved there. The lady was just a beautiful soul, very kind and thoughtful. It was like having my grandmother come to visit. She said it was her mother's birthday that day, and she invited my husband and me down to her home to meet a cousin who had bought the house from her mother.

Earlier, when I spoke about the vision, I saw myself sitting at a big table with a food buffet. Now I'm in the house. While we were all sitting down just about to eat, I was telling them about my vision, but there were potatoes on the table in my vision, and her son jumped up from the chair and said, I forgot to put potatoes on the table. We all laughed. They were potatoes with herbs in them.

I enjoyed the amazing journey Spirit had brought us on. I feel very grateful for the experience and for meeting such a lovely family that welcomed us into their beautiful home. God bless them all. It was the year 2000, a magical time that happened.

A Mother Dying Of Cancer

A few years ago, I ended up in the hospital with kidney stones. While there, I chatted with the girl in the bed next to me. She told me her neighbour was in the cancer ward and dying with only weeks to live. She has two little kids, a boy, four years old and a three-year-old girl.

The children came on the same day. Watching two little children about to lose their mother was heart-breaking. I had a box of sweets, and I told them I couldn't eat all the sweets by myself and asked if they would help me. The children were delighted. I told them a story I thought would give them an understanding of Heaven to help them when their mother passed over.

I told them there were many babies in Heaven, tiny babies, and they cry a lot because they have no mummy and Holy God was looking for a new mummy to go to Heaven, to love and mind the babies. And the mummy has to be special and kind. Holy God was looking for the best mum in the world who would give the babies the best hugs and kisses and they won't be so sad crying all the time.

It would be great for a special mum to go to Heaven to help the babies. The children agreed.

When the mum died, I felt the children understood their mum was the best mum to go to Heaven.

When I went to get my kidney stones removed, they were already gone. God brought me into the hospital to meet those children and prepare them to accept their mum's passing.

Angels Opened My Eyes

I have had faith for many years, and I surrender to trust. I had been smoking for years and started getting a burning sensation in my throat. It felt like my neck and my lungs were filling up with lead. It was a horrible feeling. I was worried, even though I could not give up smoking. I was very addicted.

I would hear the Angels say to quit smoking for over two years, but I fought it. I liked smoking, and I didn't want to give up.

I was in Spain, standing outside the apartment where we were staying. I heard the Angels tell me to stop smoking. I told them I was on my holiday, it was my body, and I didn't want to quit smoking that week but would do it when I go home the next week. I was being stubborn.

As I stood at the top of the hill, life left my body on one side. Still standing, I couldn't move. I couldn't move my right leg as I would have fallen to the ground. I said "Okay, Angels, I'm sorry, no more smoking." The life force energy came back into my body. I said "Thank you, Angels."

A few weeks later, I went to see a psychic. In my reading, she said she saw I was to have emphysema, and then she stopped and told me that I seemed to have passed that illness. She had never experienced that in a reading before.

God bless the Angels for looking after me.

Mum's Passing

I spent the nights in the hospice for a week where my mum was in and out of consciousness, slowly passing back and forth. My mum's brother and sister had passed, as did her parents many years ago.

While I watched Mum drift in and out of consciousness, I started getting a vision of her getting ready to go and meet them. First, she said she would go to her brother, and then she started looking at her watch. Then, she changed her mind and said, "No, I will see my sister." She looked at least twenty years younger.

I would see similar visions over the week, generally tidying the kitchen and carrying on usually. At that time, I would see my Mum smiling over at them across a corridor, saying "I'm coming," and saying "Hi, how are you?"

She was thirsty, so I wet her lips with water, and her mouth would be moving as if speaking. I brought my dog into the hospice and I was lying on the seat with the dog on my lap. I was starting to get waves of energy coming up my legs. Then, I felt an energy move through my body. It felt like it was getting stronger. Then it would get stronger and stronger. I told the Angels not to let the energy go into my heart, and then it gently went around my heart and calmed down. This was happening for about an hour. I knew my mum would have a heart attack as I had experienced a similar sensation years ago in another situation. I could see the colour changing in her face, going a little blue, so I rang my cousin and said "Come now. I think it won't be long, that Mum has started to pass."

My cousin arrived within half an hour, around 5 am. The nurses came in to turn my mum, and I asked them not to. The nurses said she was okay and that she was peaceful and comfortable. I started to tell them that she was going to pass soon. They didn't believe me. As they moved her, her breathing stopped for a few minutes, and she slowly started to breathe again. Then they said maybe we would turn her later.

I stood by the bed and said "Mum, it's OK. It is time to go to Our Lady. She is waiting for you." She always had great faith in Our Blessed Mother. In the last few weeks of her life, she was angry she didn't want to die, and I said I would pray, so every night, going into the early hours, I would pray at 3 am. I always said the prayer of the Chaplet of Divine Mercy. I would play it on YouTube, sing gently by her bed, and say the Rosary. The room was calm and peaceful, and when the nurses came into our room, the peace was very powerful. They felt it too. One nurse described it. She said, "It feels as if time stood still in this room." Mum was gently drifting as her breathing slowed down. She passed very peacefully at 6:15 am. The nurses brought my cousin and me some tea and toast. Just as I was about to drink my tea, I could hear my mum saying, "Did I frighten you?" I smiled and said "You did, but everything is OK now."

Within a few days, we had the funeral. Mum didn't want anyone to see her, only close family and friends. I just put the funeral details on the paper and kept it private, as she requested. Mum was laid out in the coffin. She had a great eye for fashion, and I put her lovely chunky pink knitted cardigan on her and a matching scarf. As I sat with my cousin in front of the coffin, I felt a little push on my arm then I heard "I don't look too bad, I supposed." I smiled and said "You look good, Mum."

A few days later, we were coming down the street, and I sensed my mum meet us on the road. I asked Mum to come into the car with us, and she did. Mum started crying, saying she missed us and didn't want to leave us. It was just heartbreaking. My cousin and I cried. It was just devasting, and our emotions were so raw. She thanked us for looking after her and telling us to look after each other. She stayed for half an hour and then her presence dissipated. We were delighted she came, and I feel very blessed that we were able to chat with her. That time was very precious.

Merlin, My Guide Face In A Crystal

Many years ago, when I was starting my journey of spirituality, I suddenly got it into my head to get a crystal. I wasn't drawn to crystals before that, so I bought a quartz crystal. I felt I had to get it.

Merlin was one of my Guides. He is playful, funny, into mischief, and a wizard. My friend Dee would often channel him. To be part of that was just magical. I was always fascinated by channelling because anything can happen. While Dee was channelling, I asked Merlin if I could see him.

I showed Dee and Joe the crystal. Then Joe said Merlin wants to put something into the crystal for you. I thought, great. I asked Joe what he put in. He said he didn't know as it was for me. When I held the crystal, I felt an energy sensation, like someone was gently brushing inside my head.

The next day I could see a vision of Merlin. His energy felt very powerful. I saw him every day for the rest of the week as if he were standing before me. I saw him the second week, a bit lighter and starting to fade. Going on to the third week, fading more and more, and he just faded till he was gone. I was stunned. That was just amazing. Again, I was just fascinated.

How could this happen?

I got my wish. I wanted to see him, and I did. He gave me a vision of it. How amazing is that? It was just incredible.

The Angels Asked Me To Write A Book

The Angels have been asking me for years to write this book. I didn't feel confident writing it and always put it on the long finger.

One morning I was going downstairs and got a very sharp pain in my hand. It really hurt. I asked the Angels why did I get the sharp pain.

Then I heard that they had been asking me to write for many years, and I had not done it. I could tell they were not pleased with me. They reminded me they spent many years connecting me with many people and to write all the stories over the last twenty years as I had experienced so much and to share these experiences and special moments that my faith carried me through.

An Angel Painting The Ear Ring

I want to tell you about Mark, a friend who is great at painting but never seems to have the time to paint. I have always encouraged him, and I would always talk to him about the Angels.

We were chatting one day, and I asked if he wanted me to ask the Angels for someone to help him. He wanted to know how I could do that. All I had to do is ask, so I did. I called on the Angels and asked for a creative Angel good at art to help Mark.

A little Angel came, and she sat on his shoulder. "When you want to paint, all you have to do is call on her to guide you, and she will inspire you."

He laughed at me and said "Really?"As you can tell by this story, he is not the best believer.

So, I told him to believe something will happen, and she will show you she is there. His Angel's name was Wendy.

He was going out to his apartment in Spain a few weeks later and while at one of the markets, he bought a little statue that was so small it fitted nicely in his hand. He thought it was very unusual. He started to get out his paints and called on his Angels to help him.

As he painted the statue, he wondered how he could paint the detail of her earing as the ears were so tiny. He didn't have a paintbrush small enough, and the design was shaped like a little S on the earring.

It was late so he went to bed and the following day, the S letter's design on her earring was painted. He couldn't believe it. He asked how this could happen. There was no one else in the apartment.

I reminded him something would happen. He could not believe it. He started telling his family. He said they were going to think I was mad. I just smiled at him, saying "I always tell you about Angels. They are looking after us."

A Hundred Euro Note

While I was out driving, I passed a school for blind students. I felt strongly connected with it, but I didn't know why.

Over the next few weeks, I kept seeing it in my mind. I asked Spirit why they kept showing me this place and what was the significance?

Spirit showed me a one hundred euro note. "You'll get a one hundred euro note and take it to the blind school." I said "Yes, of course." I asked "Who do I give it to?"

I was told to go to the school where I would be guided to give it to the right person, so I went there. There was a Charity Day going on there, and I was walking to a table; many people were sitting around it. I felt a pull to a woman sitting at the table. Somebody asked whether they could help me. I said I wanted to talk to the lady that just stood up. I felt a strong connection towards her. She directed me to her.

I said "Hello. I need to speak to you." I told her, "Our Lady had asked me to come and see you, and she has asked me to give you this, handing her the one hundred euro note."

She just looked at me and said "Oh my God, that is amazing. I was only praying to Our Lady this morning, saying that if I just had a one hundred euro note, we would break even and keep going." She said "I can't believe you just walked in here and gave me a 100 euro note." It's a miracle Our Lady came through for me.

She was thrilled and started telling people around her. "Everything is going to be okay; my prayers have been answered."

She asked me who I was and I said "Someone just passing on a message from Our Lady." She kept saying "Thank you," and it was just amazing.

She was so grateful. I also felt grateful that Our Lady asked me to give her the money. It was a privilege. I quickly left. It felt wonderful to be included in the blessing to give.

My Body Aged In Front Of Her Eyes

One of my healing friends rang me asking if we would swap healing. I agreed as I love spending time with my spiritual friends.

She lay down, and I started doing the healing. After a while, she kept looking at me, asking if I was alright. I told her I was but she was unconvinced.

I asked her why wouldn't I be and was shocked when she said, "I don't want to scare you, but your face aged right before me." I said, "Really? I didn't feel any different." She said I looked old. All I said was "I wish you had told me to look in the mirror." I would have loved to have seen myself old. I thought we must have been clearing energy from past lives.

Twenty-One-Year-Old Beautiful Girl Was Killed

Many years ago, I was reading the local paper. There was a small picture of a beautiful girl who had been killed quite near where I was living.

There was just something about her, a lovely looking girl with her whole life ahead of her. I could feel a strong connection with her. She just pulled at my heart.

I was going to my friend Ray's home the next day. I brought the newspaper with me to show them the picture of this girl as they are healers. Ray said we would bring her into the healing room and help her pass over.

He said that even though she was dead, she was in shock. She looks at herself but doesn't know she is dead and a lost soul with no direction. I never heard of that before. At the time, I didn't know a lot about healing as I was at the start of my spiritual journey.

They lived five hours drive away from me. It was late in the evening, and I was tired from the drive. We all decided we would do a meditation the following day.

We all got up bright and early in the morning to start our meditation. Ray said we would build up the energy in the room and bring her in. We started the energy building, and Ray brought the beautiful girl into the room. I told Ray I would love to see her, but I didn't have the vision gift then.

Ray said to me, "Don't worry, she will hear you. What do you want to say to her?" I asked her if she would touch my hands, and she did. She touched all our hands. Her hands felt cold and damp. I could hear her say "Thank you" many times.

Ray said, "Christ, Our Lady and the Angels just came into the room" as we all sat in a circle. You wouldn't hear a pin drop. The room felt so peaceful and calm, as if time stood still.

Then I was stunned at what I heard next. In a very upbeat energy, as if we were at a party meeting friends, I could hear, "Hello, how are you, welcome home, it's great to see you, we had been so looking forward to seeing you."

Christ, Our Lady and the Angels were excited to see her saying, "Did you have a good time, are you tried? It's great to have you home."

Well! I didn't expect to hear that. They were all so loving and caring to her. I was stunned. It was an amazing experience. I felt so lucky and grateful to be there. It was just so beautiful and incredible.

Then Ray saw a white light that lit up the room, and they just soared up to the heavens, and the room's vibrations changed. The room felt so peaceful.

Whatever fear I felt about dying, I know I will be in safe hands when the time comes.

Gary's Message From The Angels

I rang Gary, a friend of mine and told him "The Angels are telling me you need to go for a healing. They said you are going to have a stroke." He laughed at me, saying, "We're all going to die. I don't believe in Angels."

"That's okay" I said, "Just remember you are getting messages. They are trying to help you, and you should listen to them. This can be prevented" but he didn't believe me.

Many years passed, and I heard he had been very sick and returned to live with his family. I rang to see how he was. He said he had a really bad year.

He was going into hospital for an operation. A few days later, he got a stroke while under the anaesthetic and passed.

I went to the funeral home to see him. I looked in the coffin and thought I must be in the wrong place. That's not Gary, and I could hear the Angels saying to look again and to look at his hair. He always had beautiful silk hair. Yes, it was Gary. I just didn't recognize him. He had lost half his weight.

While standing there, I could see him sit up in the coffin, get up and go over to see his friend. He came from behind. He put his hands around his neck and started talking to him and pulling at him in a fun way. The man shook for a second, and I told him, "We are at your removal, Gary. He can't see you," and Gary just looked in the coffin and saw himself. He didn't know he was dead.

I spoke to his friend after asking him if he felt someone pulling at his neck. He said "Actually, I did." Then I told him that was Gary, and he told me he believed me because he always did that to him. They didn't see each other often, and that was their banter. He said now he knows he came to say goodbye.

Our Lady Looked After My Health

While praying, Our Lady came to me and said that I needed to check my tummy. I went to the doctor and asked about it.

The first thing the doctor said was "Have you pain? How are you feeling?" "I am feeling fine, and I don't have any pain." I couldn't tell her about Our Lady because I don't know if she had any faith.

She sent me for a scan, and I got the results. I had a big cyst the size of an orange. I was waiting to have the operation. Then Covid happened, and I was told I would have the operation in six weeks, which ended up being six months.

While going into the hospital, I asked the Angels if I would be okay, as I am a high risk with high blood pressure and sleep apnea. They showed me a vision of me putting up the Christmas tree. I was very grateful to get that message.

After the operation, the doctor told me we were very concerned about me. They wanted to keep me a bit longer so I had a total of three days in intensive care. Then they moved me to a ward, and I was there for a week.

The doctors came on their rounds and said we are very pleased you are going home. We didn't think you would be at the time of the operation.

I said to her that I knew I was high risk. I prayed before I went to have the operation, telling her about the vision the Angels gave me of the Christmas tree, and I asked the Angels to be there during the operation. I knew there could have been complications with my medical history. The Angels said the cyst would turn cancerous if I didn't have the operation. I just placed my faith and trust in Spirit that they would help and get me through this.

The doctor said they wished I would have told them that. She said it wasn't looking good for me. I am eternally grateful to Spirit; I do feel truly blessed.

Orbs In My Bedroom

While going to sleep one night, I could see orbs in my bedroom just floating around the room. They were orbs of my deceased partner. As I tried to look closer, it wasn't easy to see as they kept moving. It looked like a pair of glasses. How could that be? I started to take photos of the orbs on my phone. Once I took them, I magnified them. Not only did I see the glasses, I could see a face behind the glasses. It appeared to be my deceased partner.

I asked if it was him to close one of his eyes, and he did. Then I would take more photos and I could see him wink again.

This continued for about half an hour as the orbs floated and disappeared, and another would come. He didn't speak to me when this was happening.

It was late at night so I left a little lamp on, with soft lighting on the landing which makes it easier to see the orbs.

I was getting visions before my partner passed and heavenly moments. My partner and I had split up. He was drinking a lot, and I started getting little visions over a few weeks of our fun times. We always had great banter; it was a really lovely relationship.

One thing he used to do in the kitchen was look out the back window into a tiny garden surrounded by four walls. He would look left, then right, left, and right again to see if anyone was looking in the window. Then he would stand before me, catch me to dance, and kiss me quickly. Looking out the window again to make sure no one was looking – just silly fun.

Another vision I will share with you is when he was going out, saying goodbye, he would stand by the front door and ask for a kiss. If I didn't kiss him, he would go out to the car, take it out of the driveway and come back and tell me this was my last chance to kiss him goodbye. So, I had to get up to kiss him.

If I was going out, I would ask him for a kiss and he would say he hadn't time. Then he would kiss me quickly and say he had changed my mind.

There were lots of visions, lots of memories we had shared. I couldn't understand why I kept seeing our relationship play out before my eyes. Afterwards, I was told that he was sending me all the good times when he passed. He told a few of my mediumship friends this.

When he had passed, a few days later, he would come back while I went to sleep. He would talk to me. And I asked him what Heaven was like. Then I would get a vision of a bright light really strong, and feel peace in my body, really calm. And then he would say, after a while that he had to go now. I asked why, and he would say I have things to do. He was an Angelic worker. At that moment, I got a strong sense of how evolved he had become, and so humble with integrity.

The next time he came, he showed me a classroom like in college with all the different emotions written on the doors. There was misunderstood, anger, sadness, bitterness, mental issues, thoughts, judgement, forgiveness, sorrow, grief, taking one's character, deception rootless, egotistic, narcissism, and truth.

We are Spiritual beings in human bodies, on earth, to experience human emotions. He also showed me a marble swimming pool like they would have in Egyptian films long ago, with a grandeur surround.

Then I saw energy of a tall narrow shape of white light, it just landed slowly in the pool and turned into a man's body, just dipped in the pool, and he came out of the pool, and his body changed back to light and vanished into thin air and then the vision left.

He would often come and stay with me at night— the peace he would bring. I always felt very calm and safe. I could feel he was protective of me when he came. He told me about my future, that I would write books, do Spiritual work, and help people. In a life-changing way, he said he was also part of my journey. He described it as his blessing. He was so humble. It was pure unconditional love, a beautiful moment. God bless his soul and his beautiful heart. It is a very emotional moment as I remember him. It brings a tear to my eye.

Spirit Wrote My Name On My Chin

A few years ago, I was taking off my makeup and looking in the mirror as I tried to remove my mascara.

Looking closely, concentrating with my eyes, I could feel a strange sensation. I started to feel that energy in my eyes. I could see my name Christine written on my chin in calligraphy writing. At the same time, I saw an ageing wrinkle on the right-hand side of my face, which spooked me.

An Inspiration For The Name Of The Book

This is my journey to finding faith; it has been a magical life, and so much has happened. One day I called down to Maire, my friend living in Blarney. I told her about writing a book, but I didn't know what to call it. I wanted to have the word faith in the name of the book.

As faith has improved my life, I don't feel alone anymore. When I was much younger, I always felt something was missing, and I didn't feel complete.

Maire suggested we go to the church for inspiration. There was a tall stand with a book open on it, and I read it. It said the words My Journey To Finding Faith in the second paragraph. I didn't have faith for many years, and everything I wrote in this book started to happen. It has been a journey of faith. I am very grateful for all the blessings and all the amazing people that were guided into my life. It is beyond belief so many messages have been given over the years.

A Connection Of Energy That Went Through Me

Nuala, a girl I know, asked me about a friend going through a difficult time and looking for guidance with questions and answers.

While I tuned into her, my body's energy started to wobble and shake a little, losing balance.

Weeks later, I met her with her friend. I knew she was the friend she was asking me about as she struggled to find her balance.

The messages are too personal to write about but she got her question answered to her gynaecological problems.

I didn't stay too long in her company, as I felt very ill, and her energy completely drained me. I am an Empath and would like to explain what happens to an Empath, just to give you an example.

I visited my aunt in hospital the day after she had an operation for cancer. My body soaked up the pain of the operation like a sponge. I felt really ill and because of the cancer, my body was completely drained of energy. It was extremely difficult to walk out of the hospital. Feeling the energy of the anaesthetic, I felt a little disorientated in my head and my body was very fragile. I was in a lot of pain and unable to drive from the connection of energy that went through me. There are many Empaths in the world today. By being in their company, we pick up on their stress, anger, and grief.

Another example is when I accompanied my friend to a funeral of a young person. I didn't know anyone there. I constantly cried for four months, feeling devasted, being an Empath picking up on everyone's grief.

The only funerals I will go to now would be very close friends and family. The grief and sorrow is too much for me to cope with.

Passing A Guy On Crutches

I had just parked the car and walked a few minutes to cross the road. I was walking past someone using crutches when I got a really bad pain in my foot. I couldn't put my foot on the ground, and literally, I had to hold on to the wall, and try to get back to the car, and wait till the energy of the pain got lighter before I could drive home. The same day it was really windy with torrential rain. The joys of being an Empath.

Miracle On The Fairy Fort

I went on a spiritual retreat in Mayo. We did a meditation and I got the message to go to the Fairy Fort as the Angels wanted to show me something. I was wondering what that might be.

I went there with a few friends and as I stood there, I got this feeling to turn around and look up in the sky. I could see raindrops falling on me, but as I looked closer, there wasn't any rainwater in the drops. We were putting our hands out and touching them. It was magical to see.

As we chatted about it, we could see people walking around, talking with each other as clearly as if I was in a village yet looking at it in the sky. Then I saw a very tall man in the sky. He was miles long. It was an incredible experience to share this with all my friends.

Man And Woman With Glasses

Many years ago, I was watching TV. It was late – around one in the morning. I have a mirror in the hall, and as I walked past it, I noticed I looked exhausted. I had dark circles under my eyes. Looking at my face, I could see a man's face with glasses and a woman's face with glasses. I could see crosses on my face, and I saw a woman wearing glasses with her hair in a bob. She was wearing comic glasses for three eyes.

The next day I wrote everything I saw in a little notebook and thought no more about it. Months later, I met this gifted lady. She told me my third eye was opened, and I needed healing. She told me she wouldn't do it as she was taking time out. She had her own issues to work out. She told me she would take me to a healer called Fred she knew, and this man lived on a Fairy Fort.

When I got out of her car, she called to the woman that was Fred's wife and said "What do you think of my glasses June?" When I saw Karen with the glasses on, she was the woman that appeared on my face with the 'jokey' glasses on. I was shocked. I told her what I saw and showed her the little book. Fred looked at the book. Karen is the woman with three-eyed glasses. Fred was the man with glasses, and his wife June had glasses. And then I told him about the crosses I saw. He said the crosses are vortex on the Fairy Fort. He explained everything in my notebook.

Fred took me up to the Fairy Fort, as there was energy in the ground to heal organs in the body. I told him that in my sitting room over the fireplace, there was a girl's face on the wall, and it looked like she had scars on her neck around the throat area. She had long hair, and it was all so strange.

Then I saw visions of hills and mountains and green land for miles. Fred told me to turn around. The vision I had, now I was standing in the middle of it. Oh my God, it was breathtaking.

When I told Fred and June about the girl with the scars, June said "Oh my God, that's Sheila Murphy. She fell off a cliff in the Kerry mountains. A doctor was walking and found her and saved her life."

June went to the hospital to see Sheila and would put crystal stones under her mattress to help her with her energy. June said "Maybe we should bring you to Kerry to see Sheila and see what would happen." I was just after finishing Reiki 2 with no great knowledge of healing.

I spoke to my teacher, who taught me Reiki. She did some channelling and told me I was to do a healing on her. All I had to do was go to her and sit there to send healing to her. I felt out of my depth. I had just finished a Reiki class and knew little about healing. My teacher said I was not to worry. The work that would be done on Sheila was Soul Retrieval work. I didn't know anything about it. My teacher said for me to go there once a week and send healing while there, and let God do the rest. She reminded me I was just a channel and to see what happens.

Sheila hadn't spoken since the accident, so I went to Kerry every week for nearly twelve months. and the nurses would bring Sheila into the church for healing.

It was a hard journey there – two hours round trip every week, and I would spend one and half hours with Sheila. I would talk to her all the time. She would blink once for yes and twice for no.

The first communication had been set up with us. It was always difficult because she didn't want to look at me or even make eye contact. I always felt she was trapped in between worlds. It was so very sad.

I was always so tired when I drove home. I could hardly stay awake. I would sleep for three days exhausted and have two days to get my housework done, go to the hospital, come back, and sleep for three days. That went on for twelve months.

One day I said, "Sheila, you know you could learn this healing and give me a hand doing it. All you are doing is lying there. At least you could be doing something good." One day one of the nurses came into the church to say a prayer. Again, I would say, "Why don't you try and talk, make an effort. I have been coming here for a long time. You won't even try and do some good to help anyone." I told her to at least make an effort. I said, "Please try; I am trying to help you. Can you help me?"

She spoke for the first time in a year and said, "No, No, No." The nurse heard her, and I was just stunned. I told Sheila to talk to me. She just stared through me and never spoke again to me. I don't know if she is alive today, but when she said "No, No, No" I remind myself that she had free will.

The news spread around the hospital like wildfire. I wonder how her life would have been. Her mother and brother have addictions to drugs and drink, while her father is brokenhearted. He came to see her every day. Would she have made an effort if they were not addicted to drink and drugs?

It is a very sad story. The nurses would have often said that she lost her will to live. She would have been in a wheelchair. All she could have depended on was her dad. Addictions in families are such a difficult illness to live with.

Daisy Doll With A Blessing For Me

Daisy Doll was my little Yorkshire Terrier dog. She was a rescue dog. She had been taking medication for fluid in her heart and lungs for a while and was the most beautiful dog – full of love and always giving cuddles and kisses.

Her foster parents, Paul and Sally, just adored her and would often mind her. They lived one hour's drive away and would call to me to collect her and take her back to their beautiful cottage, her second home, and Daisy Doll loved them both so much.

Daisy Doll had a terrible life being kept in kennels for breeding, and her poor little back and back legs were bad from being stuck in a cage for years. When I think of the cruelty she suffered. Poor baby, she was just so tiny.

When Daisy Doll came to me, her fur was very thin, and she was so thin. Paul said they didn't think she would live. They both were so upset the day they gave her to me.

Back then, we decided to keep in touch, and they would take her when I would go away on a holiday or for a weekend. Paul and Sally said she needed lots of love as they didn't think she would make it.

When I brought her home, I fed her scrambled eggs, chicken and beef stew to get plenty of protein into her, to make her stronger and olive oil to help with her coat. Within six months, she was doing well.

I was going away for a few days, and Paul and Sally were going to mind her. When they called, they looked at the dog and said, "Oh, you got another dog" and asked where Daisy Doll was. I said "That is Daisy Doll." They couldn't believe it was the same dog. They noticed a significant change in her.

When she saw them, she was so excited and would jump out of my arms and couldn't get to them fast enough. She just loved them. I always said she had three people that just loved her so much.

When Daisy Doll got a stroke, it was awful. She couldn't stand up. I rang and told Paul, and he met me at the vet, as it would be cruel to let her suffer. Paul held her for her injection, and she passed very peacefully. I couldn't stay – it was too upsetting knowing I had to let her go. I just wanted to remember her alive. I felt devasted missing her, and I just loved her so much.

I went out to the car, and as she passed, she came to me in Spirit to tell me she loved me and would look after me. That night was so hard without her – my baby doll. I was sitting on the chair thinking of her, and her spirit came back to me, and she said she was free, no more pain, telling me she loved me and thanking me for loving her, saying she had the best life, and I wasn't to be upset. She went on to say she was going to reincarnate into a little girl, and I would meet her again. And she said she would be working with people in wheelchairs, giving them lots of love like I gave her.

In the weeks leading up to her death, I kept hearing that I would be rewarded for the kindness I gave, and I would say to Spirit that I didn't need to be rewarded for that. Many people are kind, and I didn't think any more about it.

Spirit told me to get my tummy checked out. I went to the doctor, and I was referred to a specialist. I was diagnosed with a fatty liver and told to diet. A year passed, and Spirit told me I had cirrhosis of the liver.

Chatting to one of my psychic friends, I asked her to see what she thought as I was feeling under the weather. She asked Spirit for clarity on this. We were told to check back with my doctor. So, I returned to the doctor to get my blood done and waited for the results. I was getting messages from the Angels telling me I wouldn't die or have to have any operation but that I did have cirrhosis of the liver.

Spirit told me I would be cured of chronic pain which I had for years. I thought that's why they said I would be cured in time, but I didn't expect what was to happen next. Daisy Doll returned and said, "You're going to be okay, don't worry."

I went to the doctor for the results of the blood test. They had come back clear. How was that possible after the Angels told me I would become tired and unwell?

I rang my friend and told her, and as I was chatting, she started getting a message from Daisy Doll saying she was looking after me and I wasn't going to get sick because I looked after her, and now she was looking after me. That is paying it forward.

I just was so shocked; I couldn't talk. My friend said, "Chris, you're not going to be sick." Then my friend laughed and said, "In all those years I have known you, this is the first time you have ever been caught for words."

Putting the phone down, I couldn't take it in. I couldn't believe it. And I asked Spirit for clarity on this, and I heard back "We told you that you would be rewarded for your kindness. You are getting your reward; it's a gift of a healthy liver" I just cried. I felt so grateful that I didn't have to suffer.

I am just amazed. I didn't see that coming. God bless you, Daisy Doll and all the Divine interventions that have helped me through this process. I am so grateful. Thank you so much to everyone helping me in the heavens.

Guided By A Diamond Cross

I met a woman, Rose at the Mind, Body and Spirit Festival in Cork. She was a healer and said, "I feel you should go to Mallow and meet this other healer."

I wondered why I should go to a healer. Rose had given me her number, so I thought, well, I will ring her and see what she says. I was going to London the next day. I would make the appointment to see her when I got back.

I suffered from depression – tired all the time. I had to pack to go to London. It was three o'clock, and I had an appointment in town at 4 pm.

When I spoke to her, she said that she had a three-week waiting list. I said that was fine. When I put down the phone I saw a vision of this healer holding Our Lord's feet and praying, and then the phone rang.

It was Cassandra, the healer. I told her about the vision that I had seen her holding Our Lord's feet and praying. She said that's how she heals. Then she said, I don't know who you are, but you must have some connection with the heavens.

She was told she had to see me today and had no time to do so. She said to go to my appointment in town, and she would ring me later.

While all this was happening, I worried I would be late for my appointment. As we talked on the phone, I was told I wouldn't be late and not to worry. I went into town; it was half past, and I didn't think I would make it.

Looking back on it, I felt like the Queen—all the lights kept going green, not one red light. The cars on the narrow road kept waving me on. Every car that came towards me stopped and let me through. As I drove into the car park, a car drove out. I got a car space; I couldn't believe it. I was at my appointment at 3:50 pm, ten minutes early.

To this day, I still can't believe it. I drove into town, got parking, and walked seven minutes to my appointment. How could this be possible on such a busy day? It would always take me an hour, and I arrived in thirteen minutes. That is what I call divine timing.

When I got home, I was just shattered and tired. I had a suit on me. I took off the suit as I wanted to lie down, and I could hear this voice in my head saying, you don't have time to rest, you have to go, and with that, the phone rang. It was the healer. She gave me directions and said to come straight away. It was all too much for me.

I was going to London at ten in the morning. I had no packing done. I was stressed out thinking to myself, "What am I doing, going to Mallow? I don't know the area." Thinking I would get lost. I was not in the mood and couldn't cope. With all the signs I was getting and guiding me, I knew I had to go to Mallow.

I went on the journey and it seemed to take forever. I did have directions, but I was so stressed. I got lost on a back country road and stopped the car. I asked Spirit for direction and I just wanted to go home. I had enough, sitting in the car in a crazy panic. Then I saw this very big cross light up, sparkling like diamonds. I followed the cross which stopped outside Cassandra's door, and asked for directions, not realizing I was there.

Cassandra did a healing on me. She said it was like a manhole lid around my face and neck and arms of my mother controlling me for years, not allowing me to be who I am, living in fear of my mother. I hadn't been able to put my arms up. For years they were always in pain. They felt so heavy.

She said my energy was tied up like a mummy in bondage, and all those ties around me needed to be cut to free me.

A few years ago, I got a vision of myself being buried, in the ground breathing through a straw just above the earth so I could get air. What she said about being tied up like a mummy resonated with me.

I was very grateful to Cassandra for doing the healing on me. She knew how dramatized I was when I was ready to go home on all those country roads. Her husband was very kind. He told me to follow him as he drove to put me on Cork Road.

I was very grateful to Spirit, for guiding me with the cross of diamonds to Cassandra's house. I felt very blessed by Spirit that day.

Many thanks for all the divine intervention from the heavens.

*Open your mind to the awareness while reading this story,
and through unjudgemental eyes,
observe the energetic damage of projection of negative energy.*
***

Spirit just came to me this minute, as I was thanking them and asked me to explain about my childhood and why I needed healing. I said I don't feel comfortable writing about what happened to me in my childhood, and Spirit said "Its time now to stand and walk in your truth. It will help others who have come from similar backgrounds."

When I was a lot younger, about the age of sixteen, my depression started. My mother was angry for years. Every day when I would come in from school walking in the hallway in fear, not knowing what mood she would be in. If I were five minutes late, she would slap me in the face, sometimes knocking my head off the wall.

Remembering back, I would always check to see if she would have her rings on. The slap would be worse, as her rings would really hurt the cheekbone on my face.

As a child having to clean the house, skirting boards behind the bed or chairs, my mother would run her finger along them to check if they weren't dusted properly. If she found dust on her finger, she would slap me across the face again. Shouting and throwing whatever she had in her hand. Sometimes a beating would follow. After many years of having to do housework, there was always an inspection. If whatever she told me to do wasn't done correctly, more beatings would occur—the Projection of Obsessive-Compulsive Disorder.

When I was only ten or eleven, I constantly lived in fear, afraid to talk, even to look at her, and only allowed to speak when spoken to. The only time I was free was when I was at school. The fear of my mother continued into my adulthood, up until the age of about forty.

When I attended a healer, she pointed out that I was constantly trying to get approval from my mother, and if I didn't have it by now, I never would. That healer broke that pattern then and I could pull back from my mother emotionally. My mother continued her mind games until she lost consciousness before her death because I was no longer hooked in to the mind games. I could stand back, observe her, and not be emotionally attached. As a result, I could care for her with love in the final days.

All the years of abuse caused a manhole of concrete energy projected onto my energy field, causing pain and making me feel numb. All the ties of control wrapped my body like a mummy in bondage. It's not visible to anyone, but the damage it has caused is like a carry bag of coal that weighs you down, and your body is completely exhausted from stress. And, of course, you don't see the struggle. As the energy builds over the years, your emotional body is suffocated and can't function.

My grandmother was very strict. In later years, my mum would tell me some stories about her mum being controlling and how she was raised. When I asked her why she would raise me the same way her mother raised her, she said it was to make me strong. I said "Could you not see how much you broke me? Did you not learn any lesson from how you were raised and decide to be a better mother and love your child enough not to put them through abuse?" She just said that was the way she thought it was meant to be. She didn't know any other way. That's all she knew.

I said the lesson I learned is the pattern of parenting that would have to be changed for the next generation. A child has to be loved unconditionally, not loved with conditions.

And living in fear, not allowed to talk, only when spoken to and sent upstairs to do homework in the cold while my mother sat in front of a fire. At that time, not many people had central heating back in the 1970's.

Spirit asked me to explain the energy of depression. All are suppressed emotions, some without names, where energy flows, energy goes.

All the above that I have spoken about and being beaten down by control causes depression in a child who doesn't have the freedom to express themselves.

Portraying narcissist parental behaviour, playing psychological manipulative mind games, taking one's character through devious deception. Projecting their issues because of living their altered reality spiralling, years of abuse enables the pretence of showing themselves as the victim.

Words carry so much power when anger and rage are used and projected negatively. It is very damaging to the individual's energy field. The servility of abuse caused the manhole lid of concrete, and all the negative ties of energy wrapped up like a mummy in the ground, feeling suffocated and breathing through a straw out of the earth.

I felt guided by Spirit to say this, and for everyone reading this story, to bring awareness of all emotional issues and their importance to our wellbeing. All the negative energy has to be removed. This is why going to a healer is very important for our well-being: feeling freedom and comfort in one's body.

The Metaphor Spirit is saying to explain this. It's like wearing wool socks in the winter, with a hole in them with your big toe out.

To break free of these overwhelming emotions. You can always ask Spirit to guide you to the right healer. Many healers are out there with different gifts and tools to work with.

There Are No Coincidences

I met this girl I went to school with many years ago. She invited me to her home for coffee, as she lived only five minutes away. As we sat in her conservatory having coffee, I started to feel very lonely, sad and felt like crying.

I told her this. She started to cry, saying she cries there all the time. She had been crying for years. I then felt a vibration in my chest. I told her she needed to check her breasts, as I felt she needed to.

Bless her, she got checked and discovered she had cancer, but they caught it in time. She was one of the lucky ones. Somebody was watching over her. I went to see her in the hospital. There was a priest there doing his rounds. She told the priest how she ended up there, and how I was guided to tell her to get checked.

He asked me if I could help him with questions and answers as he struggled with his faith.

I told him "Ask God the question in silence. And he will give you the answer." I thought that was better, as it gave him his privacy. Because he is a priest, it reminded me that we are all human and struggle sometimes. The first answer to the questions was "The book is closed on that one" and the second answer was "It will happen in six months." He told me, the answers he got, helped him with his faith.

Angels Help A Little Girl

At Gatwick airport, feeling a little hungry, I wanted to get a quick burger and chips at the restaurant. It was very busy and there was nowhere to sit. Just as I walked in, a man got up and left the restaurant so I asked the man sitting there if he would mind if I sat down. He started making room for my tray.

We just started chatting, he was polite and asked if I was going on holiday, and I said yes, that I was going to Alicante. He said he was in Alicante last year and had just come back. He had got a phone call to say his daughter had been in an accident and was lucky to be alive. Just as he said that, I felt a chest pain around my heart. I could also feel like my heart had clipped into it. I felt a scar was there.

He then said she had open heart surgery.

Spirit started to show me, and I described it to him. Then Spirit showed me it needed healing light put into his daughter's heart.

He told me that his daughter always had Angel wings and fairy dresses and had great faith in the Angels today. Her doctor said she was very lucky to be alive, and somebody must have been looking after her because of her injury. She should have died. I told this man the Angels want to help your daughter again.

"The Angels are asking me to ask you if they can put healing energy into your heart. When you get home, can you call on your Guardian Angel, then call on your daughter's Guardian Angel and ask Angels to transfer the energy to help heal your daughter's heart?

Once it is transferred to your daughter, you will feel a change come over you. There are Angels here right now, and they are asking me to ask you to put your hand out in front of you now, and the Angels will put a sensation feeling into your hand. It's energy."

The man could feel tightness at first, and then he got a feeling as light as a feather. That's how he described it, and then a heavy feeling. The Angels then said once you feel this, you will know your daughter's heart will be healed.

The healing insulation energy will keep your daughter's main artery vein to her heart. He was amazed at what the Angels said to him because his daughter had a few operations to fix the vein which kept failing. The insulation healing energy would keep it from failing again.

The man said he didn't believe in Angels before this, but after what just happened and what he felt, how could he not believe it?

He kept thanking me, and I told him to thank his Angels; they do the work. I am only a channel. All I do is collect information and deliver it.

My flight was being called, and I had to go. "God bless you," I said to the man. "And God bless your daughter's faith."

I was home three weeks and I received a message from the Angels telling me the transfer from the father's heart to his daughter's heart was complete. I smiled and thanked the Angels for telling me. It was music to my ears. God bless all the Angels for their work. What would we do without them? I am so grateful to be a part of this journey. The Angels came through for his daughter.

Hand In The Air

I was out for lunch with my partner, and this very nice young man was serving us at our table. It was his twenty first birthday. His father was coming to collect him as he was having a party at his house that night. We have been going to this restaurant for years, and he would always come and say hello, and give us a table in his section.

He is a very spiritual guy. He carries a lot of white light in his energy field. A gentle soul, he loves Angels and would always talk about them.

He was telling me, he didn't get on with his mum, that she suffered with her mental health, and there were tears in his eyes. One day, he told me he never did anything right in her eyes and how he struggled.

With his mum's depression, I said "Can you imagine how your poor mum feels?" I told him depression is an illness, and she can't help the way she is. Bless her. He said he hadn't thought about it from her perspective and thanked me for saying it.

He finished work within half an hour. He said he told his dad he had met us and how we believed in Angels. He said his dad would like to meet us and asked if he could bring him to our table. "Of course, you can," I said.

He introduced us to his dad, and he joined us. He was tall with very good-looking black curly hair; his son Mark looked like him.

We were chatting to his dad and I said how Mark is a spiritual guy. He must be so proud of him. The minute I said he was a spiritual guy, it triggered him. His father said he often talks about me and how I love the Angels. Who did I think I was talking about Angels and talking about reiki healing? He said I was filling his son's head with rubbish.

He said he didn't believe in Angels. Then he said I was weird and a charlatan.

I had said to Mark, his son about asking for an Angel to help with his exams and telling him how Angels can help me get a car parking space.

He told me to stay away from his son and that I was nuts and a crazy woman. I asked my Angels and Guides, if they were listening to him. He was annoying me. I asked them "Could you pull one of his curls or give him a little slap?"

I just said "Being spiritual isn't everyone's cup of tea, how Angels are around us, and when we invite them into our lives, they will come and help us." I then said, "I am saying this because it is true. I know you don't believe me, but they help, as I have had many experiences." I was looking at him while I was saying this. I could see his left hand going up in the air slowly. I wondered why he was doing that, but I didn't say anything,

Then he looked at his hand and looked at me in total shock. He said "What are you doing to me?" I burst out laughing and thought it was very funny. That made him worse. I said "I was sitting across the table from you and didn't touch you." He said he couldn't put his hand down.

Then again, he got angry with me, telling me to put down his hand. He said he had to drive home; you should have seen his face. I said very calmly, "If you want to be able to put your hand down, I suggest you apologize to the Angels. You can say it in your mind. They are just giving you an experience to show you they do exist."

He continued for another twenty minutes or so, telling me to put his hand down. I kept saying he had to apologize to the Angels. He started to get quiet, and his hand slowly came down.

Maybe you might believe in Angels and Guides now. He looked at me as if I was crazy. I just smiled quietly to myself and said thanks to my Angels and Guides.

You know, I felt very blessed. Spirit supported me.

On the way home, I laughed a little more with my partner. He said that man is correct; you are crazy. I said, you're right; I am. You have got to admit that it was funny.

People sometimes don't realize the Angels do have a sense of humour.

Christmas Dinner At A Friend's House

I was asked to have Christmas day dinner at my friend's mother's house. There were at least twenty-five people there, if not more. I felt a strong pull towards my friend.

We were chatting about the wonderful dinner, and I started getting messages for her. I began to say "I am being told by the Angels you made someone very happy on Christmas Eve, you did something small for someone, but it meant a lot to them."

She was quite taken back when I said it to her. Then she told me she was walking the street in Cork city. She could hear a voice in her head saying "Don't walk down that road. Go over there in a different direction." She said the voice in her head was very strong, guiding her.

She saw a Polish girl begging on the street as she looked into her eyes. They looked so sad, it was freezing cold, and she was only about fifteen years old.

All she could think about was it could have been her daughter sitting in the cold, all alone. She said the sadness she saw in her eyes would never leave her. She went in, bought her a burger, chips, and a hot drink, and gave them to her.

She kept thinking about her, and how she always took for granted she had a home. And thank God she had. She said she didn't realize how blessed she was till she saw that girl.

I Thought I'd Get Lost In Dublin

I was driving to Dublin with my friend to do a healing course. I don't know my way around Dublin because I have only driven through it but never stayed or shopped there.

I kept driving. My spiritual friend said to me "I'm glad you are driving, as I don't know my way around Dublin". I said that I didn't either, but I felt I should keep going, and we could stop and get directions to the hotel once we got through Dublin city centre when we got onto a quiet road.

We did stop and asked someone where our hotel was. I can't remember the name of the hotel as it was such a long time ago, over fifteen years.

We stopped the car. We asked where the hotel was from here. Could we get directions? The person we asked said "It's over there on the corner. You can't miss it; it would take less than a two-minute walk."

The two of us looked at each other in shock. We both laughed and said that's so amazing. I had just driven there, not knowing where I was going. Angels guided me.

I thanked the Angels, and the message I heard back was to always trust.

Lost Blackbird

I was staying in Limerick with my friend Kay having a quiet night, when her neighbour knocked on the door. She was very upset.

Her mother always feeds all the birds. A few months ago, she recused one of the birds and looked after it. The bird escaped and wouldn't have been able to fly for too long as the bird's wing was still healing.

The neighbour's daughter was trying to find the bird and asked my friend if she could look in her garden if the bird landed there. It was getting late, and she was worried the bird would die.

So, I called in the Angels and asked them where the bird was. The feeling I got was the bird would be down at the end of the road, turn right and sit on a step by the second house.

We went looking for the bird that night. I was surprised not to find the bird as the Angels said it would be at the end of the road, sitting on a step by the second house.

I kept asking the Angels "Where is the bird?" I was told it would be there. It was getting dark, so we gave up looking.

The following day I was wondering was the bird okay. I asked again for Angel's help to find the bird. The next day her neighbour's daughter was on her lunch hour from work and drove down to the end of the road, turned right, and looked where I had told her the bird should be.

The bird was waiting by the second house, where the Angels told me it would be. The neighbour's daughter and mother were thrilled to have the bird back.

The next day my friend's neighbour brought a box of sweets to the door to thank me—a very thoughtful gift. So, we all thanked the Angels for their guidance in finding and protecting the bird through the night.

Energy Through Her Hand And A Surprise

I called to my friend's house one day. Her next-door neighbour had called for a coffee. She had a stroke a few years before. All the left-hand side of her body was numb, it was difficult to walk, and her hands were twisted. She had no feeling in her hand.

I closed my eyes and visualized healing energy going into her hand; she could feel it like a thread going through her hand. She called the next day; she could put on the quilt cover on her own that night. She was thrilled with that.

She was also telling me about her belly button that since the stroke, her belly button was over in her side. She told my friend a week later that her belly button was back where it should be. God bless the Angels.

Prayer And Healing For An Apartment

My cousin wanted to sell her house, and she wanted a one-bedroom apartment. I know someone who rented a one-bedroom apartment many years before, and I said to my cousin "The landlord is living nearby. Go and tell him you are looking for a one-bedroom apartment. Ask him if any are available; and if not, give him your number."

He told her any tenants he had, stayed with him for years, and they didn't leave, so she rang me very disappointed. I then asked her if she would like to live there. She said she loved it; the area was brilliant, and she loved the scenery. I said I would pray the rosary to Our Lady and the Angels. Always when I pray, my prayers get answered. She was convinced she didn't have a hope of getting an apartment there.

Of course, she did. I got a message from the Angels saying a two-bed apartment will become available. So, I rang her and told her to ring the landlord and say that you would be interested in a two-bed if it becomes available. She did, and he said he was just about to ring her as an apartment had become available, but he was very surprised as the guy renting it has been there for over ten years, and he never thought he would be the one to leave.

When she told me all this, the Angels said at the same time it would be the one-bed apartment she was getting. Then the landlord rang back hours later and said the girl renting the one-bed apartment wanted the two-bed one. He told my cousin she could have the one-bed.

She went down to pay her deposit that night, got it, and loves it there. Thank you, Angels, for answering my prayer. I'm feeling so blessed. It is a lovely apartment, and the landlord doesn't mind her having her two dogs there.

She is thrilled to be there.

Trip To London Guided By Spirit

I was going to see my mother-in-law who lives in London. Spirit told me there would be some people on the journey that I would meet. So I flew from Cork Airport to London Gatwick, wondering who I would meet.

After spending time with my in-laws, I was packing to return home to Cork. My father-in-law dropped me off at Putney Railway Station to get the train to Gatwick.

While waiting for the train, a woman came and smiled at me. She felt she had to talk to me and asked me if I was a spiritual person. I answered "Yes, I am." She said "I believe you have a message for me." I said "Spirit told me I would be meeting people, and there are messages I will channel, but right now, I don't know what the message is." Our train to Gatwick just arrived.

We both got on the train and sat facing each other at a table between us. I told her I was returning to Cork, and she said she was getting off the stop before Gatwick. We had half an hour to chat.

I asked if I could hold her hand, then called on Spirit and asked what message I needed to tell this lady. Spirit wanted to give this lady an Energetic Toolbox. As I looked at this gentle soul, there was something very beautiful about her. She spoke so softly, and quietly the energy from her was just a stillness.

She started to tell me she worked on a private yacht. She was a chef sailing the seas. She would buy all the shopping she needed for the crew and the captain and his guests. Most of the time, she would cook for twelve people whatever they ordered, from lunch to dinner, snacks, high tea, or whatever the guests would like.

She was such an interesting person. Spirit started to tell me messages for her. The first message was she was a key to opening up the energy of the sea as she sailed from port to port.

Spirit told me to open my hands, and Spirit put energetic gifts into my hands to give to this lady. An energetic sword to cut negative ties through the ocean. An energy of love to spread through the waves. An energy of purity sprinkles through the ocean to create a vibration of love and light through the sea. The energy was just so magical it just took my breath away. I felt very grateful and honoured to be a channel. It brings tears to my eyes to remember that moment.

She asked how she could use the gifts she was just given while at sea. Spirit said "The energy will know what to do while you sail." I thought that was just incredible.

We spoke about the amazing messages that Spirit had given us. And we both spoke about what we felt as if we had known each other our whole life. When we arrived at her stop, I heard Spirit say she will give you something. She took an organic body cream out of her bag and said "I would like to give this to you as an energy exchange."

I thanked her and said I wouldn't use it but would keep it as she has such beautiful angelic energy.

As she stood up, she asked if she could hug me, and for that minute, it was like time stood still, and unconditional love energy flowed through us. As we both smiled at each other, she said we were part of a miracle connecting with the sea, and all this happened on the way to Gatwick. It was an emotional moment. We both shed a tear and felt blessed to be in service to Spirit.

It truly was a precious moment. We felt like twin souls. Meeting a complete stranger, like we were connected by a spiritual oneness. Spirit brings such joy in moments like this.

It was a magical blessing.

My Pendants

I was going out to meet my friend for lunch. While getting ready, I put on my long gold chain with two pendants. One was a gold cross, and the other was Our Lady's Medal. I don't usually put them both on the chain, but I did that day, so it was well and appropriately tied. When I entered the restaurant, the clasp was opened on my chain, when I knew it was closed before that. I only walked from the car to the restaurant and the cross and Our Lady's Medal were gone. I back tracked my steps and couldn't find them.

I asked the Angels why did I lose them. The answer I got was "You are in Service." I answered "Yes, I am." Then I heard someone that lost their faith and needed to find them. Both my cross and Our Lady's Medal was their sign.

His Psychic Gift In A Scar

I saw this healer on Facebook and felt I needed to meet him. I knew there was a reason, but at the time, I didn't know what the reason was. I made an appointment to see him to have a healing myself.

We were chatting about healing energy being psychic when the healing was over. He said he had been told he was psychic, but he said he wasn't feeling psychic. Then he went on to tell me about a scar on his leg and that he was born with it. So, he wondered if it was a wound from a past life.

I looked at the energy of the scar, and I did psychic surgery on his leg. I cut into the scar energetically, and there was his psychic gift. I took it out and connected it to his third eye and Solar Plexus, and by that night, he was doing a workshop and became very psychic. He was stunned and really enjoyed working with people and able to read energy.

Guiding Hands

My friend's husband had bladder problems. He had an operation and sadly ended up with a colostomy bag. Then he went on to have two operations so he wouldn't have to have a colostomy bag, but the operations were unsuccessful.

He was feeling very down and depressed. I asked him, "Do you pray? Have your faith?" "Only sometimes" was his answer. I told him to go to have the operation again, say a prayer and trust in God and tell me the day and time he would have the operation. He rang me when he was going down, so I called on Christ, Our Lady, and all the Angels to guide the surgeon's hands and thank God the operation was a success.

Protection Of The Angel Wing

A friend of mine had a heart attack. It took him two years to get his energy back. He started a stressful new job and was beginning to struggle, so I called on an Angel to help him. The Angel came, and he put his wing over my friend's heart to protect his heart as he is very sensitive.

You know, that was such a blessing to see the Angel cover his chest with wings, and I asked for this great Angel to stay as long as he is needed.

Negative Energy And Psychic Attack

My cousin was working in a tile shop when I called to see her one day. She had her Angel cards with her. She said she left them on the table if anyone wanted to take one.

As she said that, Spirit told me a lady would call this shop looking for help, and when one did, I asked my cousin to ring me, as Spirit would guide that lady to this shop so she could be helped. The day came.

My cousin rang me and said a very stressed lady was in the shop. She said she needed help and prayed for someone to help her. She was walking past the tile shop and felt like going in. She heard a voice saying she would be helped soon.

I had just sat in the car when my cousin rang. She put the lady on the phone, and the lady told me she had some entity in her. She started crying, and she said she had not slept for days. She said she felt terrified and wondered if she would ever be right again.

I told her not to worry and to take a deep breath. I called on Spirit to do some healing and to remove the entity. We removed it while she was on the phone. She couldn't understand how it could be taken out on the phone. How was that possible? I told her the Angels can work with energy anywhere in the world. Being on the phone is not a problem for them. She was so thrilled that it was out. She couldn't explain how it felt. She had been extremely traumatized and was going to a church now to pray for me because I helped her.

She kept saying how free she felt. I asked her to light a candle for me. She said she was guided to the church to light a candle for me and to give thanks to the Heavens.

She was a very sensitive lady and could feel energy vibrations.

An Angel In A Dog

For a few years, Spirit said I would get another puppy. At the time, I didn't intend to but when Spirit says there is one coming, it is on its way, I looked up the newspaper and the internet to see if I felt an energetic connection towards any of the adverts selling Yorkshire Terrier pups, but unfortunately I didn't at the time.

I was down the village and saw a card on the pet shop window for male and female Yorkshire pups. I rang the number. The lady lived in Limerick. Just as I talked to her about the distance, her son said he was going to Cork that day for an interview and could drop the pup off to me.

I already had two little Yorkshire dogs in the car; he wanted to pet them. They are very affectionate. As he cuddled one of them, she put her little head behind his neck, and the other did the same. He then said his mother wanted the pup to go to someone kind. He said those dogs made his mind up straight away.

When I brought the pup home, my friend called to see the pup, and I knew this little pup was very angelic. I decided to call her Angel.

The minute my friend saw her, she said "Oh my God." She said she saw an Angel in my dog. What will you call her? I am calling her Angel, a perfect name for her; Spirit has sent me an Angel. How amazing is that?

One day she was trying to tell me something. It was how she kept moving her mouth. I was looking at her. Is she hungry? Does she want a drink? Then she gave a tiny bark that she hadn't done before.

Then there was a green light the width of the pup, and it grew six feet in the air and came into me like something you would see in a science fiction movie. Spirit said it was a consciousness of love and heart energy and would help me in my life.

Spirit said they needed an Angel to bring it to me. Years later, Angel got knocked down, and the nerves in her body would have little tremors and shaking all over her little body when she would sleep. After that accident, she lost her confidence. I lifted her everywhere and minded like a newborn baby. She was very fragile, and she hurt her paw. The vet wanted to amputate it, and I said no, she would be fine. I trust in Spirit. Her paw healed well; the vet was very surprised. He said she would never walk properly. The paw was severely damaged, and she wouldn't be able to walk with it, but she did, walk and run. She couldn't walk for long periods but enough to live comfortably.

I got a little suitcase with wheels for Angel, the same size you would take on a plane and she would sit in. She loved it as she got older. One day I was at the hairdresser, and she was having a little cry. I said to the hairdresser she wanted a cuddle to calm her down. I could see her look at me strangely, so I picked her up, cuddled her, and she returned to the bag. I fixed her blanket, and she went to sleep. The hairdresser said there was no way she would have believed that if she didn't see it herself. She said she was just like a baby, and she really was. She was just so precious to me. She really was a very special little girl.

Years later, when she was about thirteen, getting a little deaf, a friend asked me to go to Spain with her. I booked Angel into the kennels. She had gone there a few times before, and the lady in the kennels would leave her in her kitchen, and in the morning, she would send her down to get the children up for their breakfast.

Her children loved her, and of course, Angel loved all attention.

A car was driving into the kennels to drop off their dog. Angel ran out when she saw the car coming, thinking I was coming for her. She would always do that when I came home. She was always excited, with a big welcome.

There was a terrible accident. Angel got knocked down and passed to the Spirit World. I had only been in Spain for three days and got a phone call about her passing.

I got such a shock. I couldn't believe it. I would have come home if she were alive, but she was gone. I was brokenhearted. I had such a close bond with her.

When I returned from Spain, the lady from the kennels brought her home to me. She said even though she had died a few days, she never got stiff. Looking at her, she just looked as if she was asleep. She never developed rigour mortis.

While she was with me, her Spirit came to me. She said, look into her eyes, and I said "I am looking at you, but you have passed." She said she would reincarnate and come back to me. She then said "When I return, you will feel an energy sensation in your eyes." Within a few minutes, I could feel both eyes, with a gentle energy with many of what I would call pins and needles. It was just incredible. And I thought, how will she come back to me? How will she find me now?

***

I am just going to bring you back in time. Ten years before, when I was at a dance in Cork, a nice couple was dancing together. I felt my eyes pulled to them. I wondered why I felt that connection. I didn't speak to them; I just knew they had a nice love energy between them and thought they looked like a nice couple.

When Angel said she would come back again, I didn't know how long I would be waiting for her. About a year later, a friend of mine wanted a Yorkshire Terrier. He asked me if I would check out the internet for him which I did. but there was a shortage of Yorkshire Terriers at the time.

When I rang the number, about a Yorkshire Terrier, for sale, the woman I spoke to said someone just phoned earlier and wanted the dog. Her son has Down Syndrome, and his dog has died. The little boy was brokenhearted, and they had agreed to give him the dog.

She said she could take my number, as she would breed Yorkies for September and October next year. Getting Yorkshire Terriers is not always easy, so I gave her my number and kept looking with no joy in getting one for my friend.

The following year, I would ask Spirit how long it would be before Angel returned to me. Spirit said she would come back but now was not the time, and when she did, she would come to your door. How was that going to happen? Then I was told to trust and wait. I said "It's been over two years." I was told once again to wait and trust.

More time had passed, and just before Christmas, I got a phone call from the woman who said she would be breeding her dog before Christmas. I had forgotten about her. She said, "Does your friend still want the Yorkshire terrier?"

When I rang him, he said the back garden needed fencing, and he didn't have the money to do it as he had been out of work due to sickness, and he said the time was not right for now. He thanked me for ringing him.

I then rang the woman telling her he didn't want a dog now, but could she send me a photo of her, as she had been telling me how cute she was. I said I might like her myself. She did. The minute I saw the photograph of her, I could hear, "Hi Mum, it's me. I'm back." I was thrilled to tell the woman. "I want her, she's beautiful." I couldn't tell her that it was a reincarnation of my dog that had passed.

I asked her where she lived. It was a country town outside Cork. She told me she wanted to see my house, and she told me her dog wouldn't be going there if it's not a safe house. I gave her my address, and she brought Angel to the door just like Spirit said.

When she came, she was only seven weeks old. The minute I saw her, I had pins and needles again when I picked her up and felt an energy sensation in my eyes like in my vision. I said hello to my Baby Angel. "What about mummy hugs?" And as I held her to my shoulder, she turned her head and put it behind my neck like before she had passed. The couple that bought her said she never did that before. She would cuddle into them, but not like that.

Because she was only seven weeks old, the woman said she would hold on to her for another week with the mother. I had Daisy Doll at the time, and she was sitting at the back of my neck the way she did her cuddles. They couldn't believe how chilled out she was. She was a rescue. I got her when Angel passed. Her husband said the dog would be safe here. Just look at the other one.

Just as he said that I got a vision of him dancing with his wife at the dance earlier in the story. I said about this couple dancing and how my eyes were being pulled to them, and I didn't know why. I connected with their energy. They were the people I liked, and I thought they had a sweet love between them, and now they are in my house. Oh my God, Spirit shows me signs, and I didn't know how all this would work.

I was so thrilled to have her. She came to my door just like Spirit said she would. As she got a bit bigger, she was bold and wouldn't do what she was told. I said to Spirit she couldn't be my Angel. She is such a diva and bold and has an attitude about her and does what she wants.

I said to Spirit, she can't be Angel reincarnated. She won't do anything I tell her; she has a very different personality. That night when Angel fell asleep on my lap, I could see her little body having tremors, shaking a little bit—exactly the way the first Angel did when she had got knocked down the first time. I couldn't believe it.

It really was her. She is a pure blessing. As she has gotten older, she has calmed down a lot. She could do with calming down a bit more. Her personality is becoming more like the old Angel.

To have my Angel in a dog's body come back to me. She is loving and keeps staring at me; everywhere I go, she follows me.

When she wants a cuddle, she does this cute little thing where she hops onto my lap, and when she goes out to the garden, she has to kiss me before she goes out. I am just thrilled to have her back. Her fur has changed from black and tan, to a silver grey. She is beautiful. She is still a diva, but I love her. She is a pure blessing, my real little Angel Girl.

Master Of Ceremonies

My cousin's neighbour is working at a hotel in Cork. The hotel was having a fundraiser dinner dance, and the hotel was supplying all the food. They had sold a lot of tickets, and all the money that was raised was donated to Marymount Hospice. The neighbour asked me if I would do the Master of Ceremonies for the evening and I was very grateful to be asked.

It's a charity I would always support as I have lost friends and family to cancer. While on my way, I got a message from Spirit, saying an Angel will work through your body tonight. I would always surrender to Spirit to be a clear channel.

When I stood up to do the speech, I felt an energy sensation from the top of my neck to the bottom of my feet. It felt like I was wearing a long dress. I felt my body being zipped open. I could feel the Angel coming into my body, putting her feet into mine, and feeling her toes, knees and the rest of her body. Her shoulders, arms, and even down to fingernails, and her head felt much stronger. I could feel her whole body connect with me. I could feel a vibration moving through my throat. As I started to speak, my voice changed.

I could see both of my friends at a dinner dance, curiously looking at me. At the end of the speech, they said "It didn't sound like you. What happened to your voice?" I then told them about the Angel.

While standing, I was told that healing was happening to everyone in the room. I asked the Angel what healing was she doing for all the people. The metaphor she showed me, was all the hurt, pain and sadness, was like a frozen block of butter. Those painful emotions have been released, showing me everybody's energy was now like whipped cream. Then the Angel sent love and light into everyone in the hall.

I surrendered thanks and gratitude for all the Divine intervention and blessings.

Jenny The Bichon

A few years ago, my friend's daughter's Bichon dog was ill, and they had to put her down. Little Jenny, she was a beautiful, loving little dog. She was never left alone; she was totally spoiled. Whenever my friend was on the computer, and Jenny felt she wanted cuddles or food, she would try and sit on the computer, and of course, my friend would have to stop work. She was a little diva.

Sitting down to watch a film, I felt a bounce of energy on my lap. She told me she wanted to speak to her mum, and she wanted me to help her. I said "Who is your mum? What is your name?" She just said, "Jenny."

I have never had a dog bounce on my lap looking to connect with her mum. I had to get her number and give her a ring. I didn't know her very well.

I had a quick chat when I rang her, telling her what had happened. I asked her if it would be ok for me to connect her with Jenny, and she was open to it.

I could feel Jenny bouncing on my lap when I started to say "Jenny's here." Jenny said "Connect me." She wanted a cuddle from her mum.

She was very impatient with me and didn't want me to chat with her. Again, she said "Connect me." I then connected Jenny's energy with her mum. She wanted me to tell her she loved her and missed her while she was sitting on her lap.

She jumped up to give her a kiss and her mum just put her hair behind her ears. I said "Jenny is telling me you just put your hair behind your ears." She laughed and said she did and thought that was funny. Jenny wanted to tell her she was always there when she was feeding her baby brother and how Jenny loved her baby brother. The energy was very loving with Jenny.

She thanked her mum for being the best mum and said she had to come back to see her and tell her that.

I told her mum she could say anything she wanted to say to Jenny and in her mind, she will hear it and understand what you are saying to her. I waited a few minutes till Jenny spoke to me.

She wanted to give her mum one more squeeze, and then she would go. I helped her energy disconnect from her mum. The vision I got was Jenny jumping up and down. She was excited and thanked me for helping her connect with her mum.

Oh, bless you, little Jenny, with your abundant unconditional love.

Sara In And Out Of Consciousness

I was walking into the supermarket, and I met Margaret. I hadn't seen her for years; we went to the same school. I was friends with her and her sister Sara when we were teenagers. She was telling me about her family and grandchildren. Then she told me about her sister, now living in New York but sadly had terminal cancer. I was so sorry to hear that. She was only in her late fifties.

I said I would include her in my prayers. She was going to New York to see her sister who was in a hospice now. It is always sad news to hear about people battling cancer. It was so long since I had seen Margaret, we exchanged numbers, and I said I would give her a ring and meet her for a coffee sometime.

She rang me when she came back from New York. We met, and she gave me a lovely card from Sara thanking me for including her in my prayers. The card touched me, and I thought it was a lovely gesture.

A few weeks later, Margaret rang me. She was very upset, saying Sara was in and out of consciousness and was waiting for her husband's news.

I was watching television, and Sara came to me in Spirit. She thanked me for praying for her and put an energetic silver chain with a love heart into my hand. I thanked her for coming. I asked her if she had passed over to the Spirit world. I had just put down the phone to her sister Margaret less than twenty minutes before, and she was still alive.

She said she was still here and just wanted to come to me before she had passed to thank me and give me the silver chain for all the prayers. I hadn't seen her since we were teenagers, and she wanted to come to me as sick as she was in and out of consciousness. That really touched my heart. A few days later, Margaret rang to tell me Sara passed.

Margaret didn't go to New York for her cremation as it is such a long distance from Cork, and she felt she couldn't make the journey again so soon as her health wasn't great. On the day of Sara's cremation, Margaret said she would go to mass simultaneously while Sara was being cremated.

Sara came to me again, in Spirit, while her cremation service was being held and asked me to tell Margaret, her sister, that she went to see her while she was at mass and to say she saw her sitting next to St Anthony in the church.

After the mass, I rang Margaret and asked how she was. She was delighted I rang. She said she had felt her sister had come to say goodbye to her while she was at mass.

I then told her Sara had come to me, to say that she had been to the church to see her when she was sitting in front of Saint Anthony. She said "Oh My God, he was right in front of me."

It was great to have the confirmation from Sara. She was glad and knew she was in church and praying for Sara while she was being cremated.

Dance Lessons For A Wedding

Many years ago, at a dance class, I chatted with the couple next to me, and they were having dance lessons for their wedding.

We were dancing, and the girl I was chatting to stumbled, and I felt dizzy at the same time. We both laughed, and she said we didn't even have a drink.

I told her I got a vision of cameras and lights flashing. She said she had only recently been diagnosed with photosensitive epilepsy. She asked me if I had that too. I said "No, thank God, I am an Empath, and sometimes I pick up on people's health issues." She was astonished and couldn't believe I saw the flashing light.

She was fascinated. She said she had always had a connection with spiritually.

Our Lady In A Silhouette Of Energy

Sitting in my kitchen, I could see an energy spiralling down the ceiling. It was a silhouette of Our Lady. I was completely overwhelmed, and she asked me to pray the rosary to her. I said I would.

She said to come to Fatima to see her. I asked Our Lady if she could guide me to someone that wants to go to Fatima, and she said it was already decided.

The following night I was back at the dance class. I was chatting to the girl I was dancing with while the teacher was chatting with one of the groups.

The girl was asking me if I was going on holiday. I said only a few days ago I decided to go to Fatima to see Our Lady. She said she wanted to go but had no one to go with. I said I didn't either. We then decided we would both go together. We got the tickets online and were going within the next two weeks.

I called to my friend for a coffee and told her I was going to Fatima. We were out in her garden when I lost my footing and fell helplessly. I had to go to hospital as I sprained my ankle. My friend asked me "Are you going to go to Fatima now?" and I said "Yes I am going, I told Our Lady I would go."

I was looking forward to the trip and got on our flight. When we arrived at the Portugese airport, the holiday representative arranged taxis for us to our hotel.

This story now connects with an answered prayer. I asked Spirit to connect me with Rose.

Now I am going to bring you back over thirty-five years, I was working in a clothes shop and this girl, Rose who was working in the office, and when I wanted to leave to go to London, she offered to do my CV. She was a lovely, kind, caring, genuine person. Everybody liked her.

I had come back a few times from London. She was either on holiday or maternity leave as she had a few babies together. I kept missing her and wanted to thank her for her kindness, which helped me get a job. I was so grateful to her.

I always said to Spirit, please can I see her again before one of us dies? Over the years, when people would say they were from West Cork, I would always say,

"Do you know Rose O'Connor?" However, I hadn't met anyone that knew her.

Now, I can bring you back to the taxi at the airport, and the girl that got in the back of the taxi. It was hot in Portugal, and we were all sitting with our sunglasses on.

I asked her where she was from, and she said she was from West Cork. I said "Really? Do you know a girl called Rose O'Connor?" She said "Rose O'Connor, I am Rose O'Connor." I couldn't believe it; I asked her to take off her glasses. Rose always had unusual eyes, and I said for years I had been asking people in West Cork about you but they didn't know you. I always wanted to thank you for your kindness. I have been so grateful to you for helping me all those years ago.

And she just said, "Really? I never even thought about it." We laughed about the shop and the fun we had long ago. We chatted about the other girls we had worked with and how she had lost contact with some as they had gotten married and moved away.

We remembered a funny story: Rose had bought a cardigan in one of the big department stores and was showing it to us. We were working in a very expensive clothes shop, where many people would come to shop for wedding outfits. Rose had to go to the bank to get money to pay the wages. While she was gone, one of the sales assistants sold Rose's cardigan. Nobody noticed until we were going home in the evening, and Rose asked if anyone had seen the new cardigan she had bought. At that time, she had paid fourteen Irish pounds for it.

Only to discover one of the staff in the shop had sold her cardigan for thirty-five ninety-nine to a customer. We all laughed. We wondered whether the customer would bring it back. When she saw the department store label on the cardigan, she never did. Our boss has given Rose the thirty-five ninety-nine and told her to go and buy two cardigans for herself and get some cakes for the rest of us out of the change. That's one of our stories from the 1980s.

In one of her stories, she said they would often laugh at me. We had a big selection of hats, and a camera was in the middle of the hat section. I was only sixteen when I started to work there. Back then, there was a storage heater on the floor; you could sit on them, but of course, none of the staff wanted to get caught sitting on them by the boss.

I used to put a hat over the camera so he couldn't see us. We always had a bit of banter. We had two sets of stairs, one to the back of the shop and one at the front, so our boss would run up the back stairs when I heard him coming. I would run down the front stairs so he wouldn't catch me. The banter was brilliant in the shop.

Sometimes Rose would turn off the camera in the office when the boss was out, then run up the stairs and throw the hat over the camera upstairs. She would tell me to put on my running shoes as he would be up soon to catch me. Rose would often tell me things the boss would say, "I will catch her one of these days." We would laugh about it. Back then, our boss was the most easy-going man and a really good boss. Sometimes he would say in front of all the staff, "Do you like hats, Chris?" or if I could I get him a coffee. Our tearoom was on the third floor, you don't mind running up the stairs, and then he would laugh. If he was stressed out, Rose would tell me to take the hat down from the camera because if he caught me that day, God help me. It is lovely to remember her through our memories. She was so much fun. She had a presence about her, and she had an infectious personality.

We met for a few drinks the next night and went to a late-night karaoke bar. We did have a great night. We went up singing, her husband was a lovely man, it was my first time meeting him, and he could sing, he had a great voice. Rose invited me to her home. She said she wanted me to meet her family, and we had arranged to meet the following week. We had a great soul connection.

Ringing To Confirm Our Meeting

After the holiday, I talked to Rose on the phone to confirm our meeting. She said her son had invited her to Spain with him and his family only the day before. She decided to go with him for a week, and we arranged to meet two weeks later.

Then three days later, I got a text from Rose saying her mother had passed. I rang her back to sympathize with her, only to discover that Rose's daughter had texted me, not Rose. It was Rose that had died.

I asked Spirit to connect me with her. She then told me she didn't want to die and leave her family. She was brokenhearted. She asked me to tell them she loved them so much.

She told me to tell them she doesn't like her hair; she hates it. She liked the funeral home she was in. It was a beautiful place.

All her family went out to Spain to collect her body. Her daughter and family didn't recognise her in the coffin with her hair as it was. They had passed her and thought they were in the wrong place.

I rang her daughter to tell her what Rose had said, and the daughter said her hair was all gelled back of her face. In the funeral home in Spain, no one knew about her hair. The family asked her hairdresser to do her hair the way she always wore it, feathered around her face.

Life is so short. God bless you, my old friend. I am so glad we had the best night out and all the memories. Writing this brings a tear to my eyes. We had such a powerful Soul Connection. It was like all the years just melted away when we connected.

Fatima And Our Lady In The Basilica

We were going to Fatima on one of those bus day trips. While on the way, I could feel powerful energy in my knees and feet. My body was more relaxed, and I could feel a calm feeling coming through me. Our Blessed Mother had started healing me.

We sat for an hour or so when we got to the Basilica. Time stood still, people sat there in peace, and you would see tears fall from people's eyes. It was beautiful.

It was a privilege to be there and I got this message to pass on to everyone.

To tell people to come to Fatima.
To ask people to pray the Rosary to Our Lady,
to love and be kind to one another.
She also asked people to pray for the Holy Souls.

I said I would do that, and through writing this story, everyone who reads this will hear her message.

When we got back to Cork, I was at the doctor, and she asked me to describe the pain in my feet. I was talking to her about a few different types of pain when I went to tell her about the sharp pain. I said it's gone since

I came back from Fatima. I didn't have that pain. Thank you, Blessed Mother, for taking that from me.

I am eternally grateful I felt so blessed. I cannot thank you enough.

A Collection Of Rosary Beads

My friend got me rosary beads from Medjugorje. They were very unusual rosary beads called Stairway to Heaven. They were a navy colour. When I prayed with them, I felt a oneness with Spirit. I had them hanging in the car, but they broke so I put them in the kitchen. A couple I was friendly with saw the beads. They were big beads, and his mums eyesight was not great. My friend said that size beads would be great for his mum. So, I gave them to him for his mum.

Time had passed, and I missed the oneness energy feeling from the beads when I prayed.

The lady was in a nursing home. I told her daughter-in-law that I missed the oneness energy from the beads. The lady passed in the middle of Covid, and the beads didn't return to me.

Paul Gifted Me Rosary Beads

Paul was going to Lourdes and he said he would try and get me the same ones but couldn't find them. He got the same navy colour, and the beads he got had the most beautiful peaceful stillness energy from them. I was very grateful for the gift of rosary beads. When I prayed with them, I always felt an energy of floating peace from them.

My Mother's Rosary Beads

I had blue rosary beads belonging to my mother when she passed and kept them by my bed. I prayed a few times with them but didn't feel a connection with them. They were lovely crystal blue, and I fell asleep one night while praying with the beads. When I woke, I found the beads broken and couldn't find the link to put them back together. I needed three extra links. I asked Spirit to bring them to me.

The Stairway To Heaven Beads

My friend was going to Knock and said she would try to get the same beads. She was in the shop looking for the rosary beads and took a photo of them from her phone and showed the assistant. She said she had them, but they were gone.

My friend felt guided to a corner in the shop and put her hand on the rosary beads tucked away. You would have to search to find them, and other beads were on top.

She picked up the rosary beads that were the Stairway to Heaven ones. She smiled at the assistant and said they were waiting for her.

When she called to see me with the rosary beads, would you believe they had three extra links? Now I have the links to fix my mother's beads, and I am always grateful for how Spirit and divine intervention work, bringing me what I need.

I felt a powerful connection with those rosary beads, and when I prayed with them, I got a vision of monks praying in a monastery.

When I was telling my friend about the vision I got, she said when she was in Knock, she went to a healing mass. She said they were over twenty priests on the altar. When they were giving the blessing, she held up the rosary beads in the air.

The energy I felt in the rosary beads was the priests' blessings. Everything in my vision made sense. That was the most powerful energetic blessing. When I pray with them, I often say an extra decade of the rosary. The energy of the rosary beads feels so powerful.

The Fundraiser Group In Dublin

A group of about twenty-five people at my friend's house were gathered, hoping to raise money for a cancer charity. They always do sponsored walks, spend all night on the street, and give their time. Anything they can think of to raise money for this charity.

I started getting messages for a girl there, saying she was in a very stressful marriage. She was out of it now, her husband was very controlling, and I felt she had met someone new recently and he was a bit controlling, but not as much as her husband was. I felt it was a good relationship for her.

The new guy had to be careful with the controlling, as Spirit said she would walk away from the relationship. I said I felt guided by Spirit to say this to her and asked if this made sense to her. She was being vague, yet the energy around this relationship felt very strong. I told her I felt she would know who I was talking about as it felt so current as if he was standing beside you.

Then one of her friends burst out laughing and couldn't stop. The more I spoke about this new relationship, her friend got hysterical. She apologied for laughing and gestured for me to keep talking. I then went back to speak to the girl, and then another outbreak of laughter.

While we were eating afterwards, the girl came to talk to me, saying she was seeing someone new nobody knew about. She wanted to keep it quiet as it was early days, her marriage was over only a few months, and she wasn't ready for a serious relationship.

The girl that was laughing, her friend had figured it out that morning, and they had sworn her to secrecy. They confirmed the truth with her. She said everything I mentioned was true. They were taking the relationship slow.

A Lady And Her Son

At the supermarket, I met this lady who was a friend of a friend of mine. Her son passed some time ago and came through; he wanted to talk to his mum. He told his mum he loved her and thanked her for keeping his name alive through all the money they raised for cancer.

He said he knows she hugs his face when she sleeps at night. She then told me she had a small pillow in her bed with a picture of his face on it and cuddled into it when she slept.

I could see her son putting his arm around her neck. I told her to close her eyes as she would feel the hug.

I heard her son saying, "I am squeezing her." It's a tight hug, and his mother said she could feel him hugging her.

It was a very emotional connection, and I felt privileged to be part of her experience.

A Gentle Soul Needed Help

I was shopping with my Dad and dropped him off to meet my cousin for coffee. I was walking down the street, and suddenly there was a very heavy rain shower. I rushed into a restaurant to get shelter from the rain. A man was outside, and his clothes looked scruffy, bless him. He was probably homeless. I could see him heading towards one of the bins, and I saw him put his hand in the bin.

I asked him if he was hungry, and he replied he was thirsty and would love a drink. I asked what would he like? He said anything. I enquired if he would prefer hot or cold and if he would you like a burger and chips or a sandwich? He said, no, just a drink would be great.

I went to get the drink and gave it to him, and I saw sadness and emptiness in his eyes. He looked lost in himself, and all I had in my purse was some loose change and ten euros.

Reflecting on the day, he could have had something to eat to warm him up on such a cold day, but he had refused the food. He was so humble. I put the ten euros in his hand and said you get fish and chips later when you're hungry.

Bless him, and I always think I am very lucky to have a home. I might have been living on the street if my life had gone in a different direction. Reflecting on the day, I felt Spirit guided me to him, even the way I started talking to him as if I had known him.

I Didn't Have Faith

I called in to meet my friend for lunch. She was serving a customer, a tall, distinguished man dressed in a tweed suit. He spoke with a strong English accent. He was looking through photographs from Medjugorje.

He showed us photographs of Our Lord's reflection in a window. The staff were astonished. He turned and looked at me and said "You don't have faith, do you?" I said "Well, I don't think religion is for me."

He said, "On the contrary, my dear, it is very much for you." At that moment, I felt he was a bit strange, and then he said "God will bring you to your knees." In a righteous tone, "You are His child." I shivered when he said that to me.

We all said he was a bit eccentric when he left the chemist.

For years it always stuck in my head what he said and how he said it. I can still see him, remembering the smell of cigar smoke and every word he said. I felt it through to my soul, and I must say I felt a bit spooked by him at the time.

On reflection looking back forty years, I would have to say he was passing a message of awareness to me from Spirit. And I did find faith.

A Feeling Of Pressure In His Chest

My friend Joe felt pressure on his chest for many years. While we were chatting one day, I felt it too. He has been living in London for years. He said he has been trying to release this blockage for a very long time. Everything he has tried; over the years, it just hadn't worked. I was surprised to hear this, as Joe is one of the best healers I know.

I asked my Spirit Guide Merlin to help me. Merlin showed me this blockage in his chest. Joe has past life issues stored. There was also a lot of power as he worked as a healer in his past life. I had to find a way to separate his issues from his power. So, I used the energy to melt the issues into little steel energy balls and put a type of structure into his chest to release one little energy ball at a time. As the energy goes into that ball, energy releases the issue.

When a person feels numb inside, I saw this as an emotion with no name as the energy ball would be released, and the emotions would come through his body. He would feel mood swings, emotions, and anger, and his chest felt much better as those little energy balls were released. He said he had a lot of emotional issues releasing. It was a challenging time for him and, of course, very exhausting.

All this emotional energy took six months to release from his chest, and he was very grateful to Merlin. Joe also worked a lot with Merlin. Sometimes we need other people to help us out.

After the months had passed, he told me he was teaching meditation to a class of thirty people. His power was so strong that it put all thirty people to sleep for forty-five minutes. He was totally amazed. Sometimes we need our energy field strong to hold such power as it takes a while for our energy field to integrate into our bodies. The same as you need a foundation to build a house, I think that's the best metaphor to explain. Then, it needs to sit and pause.

Please Spread The Word And Review

Dear reader,

If you found this book helpful, can you please spread the word and share it with someone. I would also appreciate if you could leave a review about the book, if you purchased it online.

Thanks

Chris

9 781915 502322